London
June 2003

Rico

You have done so much to make our stay in
this great city both comfortable + memorable:
a home base with Steve,
special friends to look after S.J.,
supper with Richard at the Pizza Express,
a visit to Farnham,
afternoon tea with Uncle John,
+ so much more . . .

Dear, dear brother, Thank You.

Ross.

"Loads of Luv S-J"xx
Siyabonga!!

Nelson Mandela

A life in cartoons

edited by

Harry Dugmore

Stephen Francis

Rico Schacherl

ANGLOVAAL ● MINING

AVMIN

David Philip Publishers

Thanks to Dov Fedler, Zapiro, Dr. Jack, Derek Bauer and Tom Halliday
for permission to use their cartoons on the cover of this book.
Thanks to Karina Turok for permission to use her photograph of
Nelson Mandela on the back cover of this book.

Published in 1999 in Southern Africa by
David Philip Publishers (Pty) Ltd
208 Werdmuller Centre, Claremont 7708
in association with Rapid Phase (Pty) Ltd
Johannesburg

ISBN 0-86486-393-4 (Soft cover)

ISBN 086486-457-4 (Hard cover)

Reproduction by Syreline Process
Printed by CTP Book Printers, Caxton Street, Parow, Cape.

Acknowledgements

In compiling a book such as this, we've accumulated many debts of gratitude to people and institutions who have helped, instructed and inspired us along the way.

Gulietta Fafak worked unflaggingly to track cartoons and cartoonists from every corner of the globe. Her attention to detail and can-do attitude made this work possible.

Zann Hoad, who oversaw the publishing process from its inception, has shown that she has few peers when it comes to drive and determination. Her cheerful attitude kept the book moving forward.

Zapiro, aka Jonathan Shapiro, provided encouragement, leads and inspiration. His cartoons are some of the finest in this book, and his help and support are greatly appreciated.

David and Marie Philip, and Bridget Impey, Russell Martin, Francois van Schalkwyk and Maggie Davey at David Philip Publishers have been enthusiastic supporters of this project from the beginning. They have had to put up with maverick suggestions and unusual methodologies. No one could hope for a more cheerful publishing partner, or one more committed to the freeing of human potential.

Ryan Francois and Ardi Schutz have worked on the design, the cover and the look and feel of this book. Their artistry makes this book easy on the eye, and gives proper weight to the art of the cartoonists.

Many friends and academic colleagues commented on various chapters of this book. Charles Dugmore, a dedicated historian, checked facts, proofed drafts and provided clear analysis when it was needed most. Joey Monson's research was impeccable and her sense of organisation helped get the initial 2000 cartoons down to the 166 of the very best which are included in this book. Steve Kromberg and Erica Elk have supported the project from its inception and always provided the most constructive kind of feedback.

Gail Strauss inspired this book's genesis with warmth, affection and well-timed criticism. Lindsey Stevens at Rapid Phase provided the back-up and support necessary to complete this book – and so many other projects. Her sense of humour brought us through the many fearsome deadlines. Indeed everyone at Rapid Phase, and our parent company, New Africa Investments Limited (NAIL), has made this publication possible.

Each cartoonist represented in this book has something to say. Usually its something funny, or something thought-provoking. Often their cartoons are moving and poignant. The talent represented in this book is remarkable – we want to thank and acknowledge every cartoonist who made their work and their time available to us.

We particularly want to thank Archbishop Desmond Tutu for his moving forward to this book. Nadine Gordimer and Pieter-Dirk Uys generously commented on the concept of this publication.

Rick Menell, CEO of Anglovaal Mining Limited, generously sponsored the research and development of this book. Anglovaal Mining Limited continues to provide a model for corporate commitment to developing the new South Africa.

Publishing this book is our small way of expressing our thanks to Nelson Rolihlahla Mandela for his role in liberating our country, inspiring our nation, and reawakening in all of us a sense of our humanity and what we are capable of achieving.

This book is dedicated to him with love and gratitude.

Contents

Foreword

Most public relations and advertising executives would be willing to give a leg and an arm to have the product recognition associated with Nelson Mandela for whatever article they are promoting – a recognition attested to by this collection of some 166 cartoons by 54 cartoonists from around the world. Of him it could truly be said, he needs no introduction, he is so well known.

Perhaps, not entirely. You see, once when I was in San Francisco a lady accosted me and very cheerily called out, "Hello, Archbishop Mandela!" She may have been wanting two for the price of one.

Apart from this almost bizarre exception, Nelson Mandela certainly has been the most recognisable and the most sought after head of state. This is a tremendous turn-around when you think that a formidable British Prime Minister dismissed him as a "terrorist". In his own country, after eluding capture as the "Black Pimpernel", the authorities tried to turn him into a non-person. He could not be quoted; no pictures of him were allowed; and they hoped that he would disappear into the limbo of amnesia assisted by a life sentence at their top-security island prison, Robben Island.

Wonderfully for the world, nothing of the sort happened. Perversely, in the view of his jailers, his stature grew and grew until he became the world's most famous political prisoner, and from prison he seemed, like a master magician, able to transmit his spell of charm and greatness.

In 1988 I was one of the speakers at a Hyde Park Corner rally to celebrate his 70th birthday. Some 250 000 people converged on Hyde Park Corner, several thousands having walked as on a pilgrimage from the many corners of the United Kingdom. And most of that massive crowd were youngsters, many of whom had not been born when Madiba went to prison.

People feared that we would be disillusioned when he emerged from incarceration, that our idol would be found to have feet of clay. What a fantastic vindication of goodness when he emerged: all the world and her husband were glued to their TV sets because this was without exaggeration one of the defining moments of our century.

Everywhere he has been it is as if he is a kind of Pied Piper – everybody, not just children, falling under his charismatic spell. Massive crowds hang on his every word, everywhere in the world.

The paparazzi could not get enough of him. Here he was with that extraordinary willingness to forgive, with remarkable magnanimity, wearing a No. 6 Springbok jersey and driving rugby enthusiasts into a frenzy – in that one action, striking a blow for reconciliation which several speeches in a week of Sundays would not have accomplished; visiting the widow of the high priest of apartheid; and lunching with the man who had prosecuted him and his fellow accused in the Rivonia Trial. An incredible icon of reconciliation and goodness. And the world could not have enough of him.

Everyone wanted to have a photo opportunity with him – the Spice Girls, Princess Di, various heads of state and miscellaneous politicians who wanted to breathe new life into their moribund careers; the list is endless. I do not know of any other politician who has been asked to so many summit farewells, of the OAU, the Commonwealth, the EU, different countries vying to have him carry out a farewell state visit. And because of his transparent goodness and integrity, only he could have persuaded Colonel Gaddafi to hand over the Lockerbie suspects.

It is a cliché, but it is true: he is a moral giant, a colossus.

We have all been thrilled to be alive when he is around. You were proud to be a human being because of this extraordinary human being. Everyone is so happy that he has got the girl of his heart and we are thrilled that they can ride into the sunset to live happily ever after. Did I say he was well known? Well, he likes to tell this story against himself. On Robben Island he was conversing with one of the inmates and asked him why he was there. The man gave him details of his activity as a member of the ANC. Then the man turned to Madiba and asked, "Well now, what about you, why are you here?"

He is God's gift to South Africa and he is our gift to the world.

Archbishop Desmond Tutu
October 1999

Introduction

Zapiro's cartoon "Nelson Mandela, the early years", which opens this book, describes a poignantly imaginative scene: a teacher in a rural classroom comments to the headmaster about the very young Nelson Mandela: "This one can't make up his mind (what he is going to be when he grows up): Lawyer, Activist, Freedom Fighter, Prisoner of Conscience, President, Reconciler, Nation Builder, Visionary and 20th Century Icon."

Millions of words have been written about the man who was – and is – all of these personas. This book is much more about the pictures than words, or, more precisely, it is about the particularly artful combination of words and pictures, the modern political cartoon. Nelson Mandela, the most extra-ordinary South African, has inspired at least two thousand cartoons in his lifetime, and this book showcases the best of these. Fifty-four cartoonists, from more than a dozen countries, capture a part of the famed Madiba Magic with a warmth that few other mediums can match.

Finding and then selecting these cartoons proved more difficult than expected. Mandela's 27 years in apartheid jails kept him from the public eye more effectively than most might care to remember – given that he is now the most famous person in the world. Surprisingly, there are almost no cartoons dealing directly with Nelson Mandela before 1980. This reflects partly the bias of the white-owned and white-controlled mass media, and partly the effect of draconian security legislation which successive apartheid governments implemented. No images, representations or photos of Mandela were allowed from 1964 onwards. Under sections 44(e) and 44(f) of the Prisons Act (Act 8 of 1959) it was a serious criminal offence in South Africa to "cause any sketch or photograph of any prison, portion of a prison, prisoner or group of prisoners" to be published. More than a hundred other laws limited freedom of speech and freedom of the press in South Africa in some way.

But a great thaw began in the early 1980s as resistance to apartheid intensified. From about 1980, the names of the African National Congress (ANC) and its imprisoned leader were systematically revived by an energised and reorganised ANC. The formation of the Release Mandela Committee in 1981, a conspicuous part of the movement to rally support for the ANC's cause around the persona of Nelson Mandela, marked an important turning-point in the history of resistance in South Africa. From this time on Mandela re-entered the public landscape and he and the ANC started to attract more generous media coverage. The first cartoons about Nelson Mandela begin to appear at this time.

Human memory is forgiving, seeking as it does to accentuate the positive, and dull the pain of past realities.

Many of the cartoons from the pre-1990 era featured in this book have been selected to remind us of exactly how cruel the apartheid system was, and how profoundly it affected the lives of every South African. As Allister Sparks writes in *Tomorrow is Another Country*, his brilliant account of the secret negotiations which led to Mandela's release and the ANC's unbanning:

> "Slavery debases master as well as slave. The warder becomes prisoner in his own jail; he is never free from the business of oppression and confinement. So, too, in apartheid South Africa, where white and black had been bound together in a web of mutual destructiveness. Apartheid, brutalizing the whites as it destroyed the self-esteem of the blacks, robbed both of their humanity."

Nelson Mandela's singular contribution to South Africa was to return that stolen humanity to a broken nation and, in so doing, inspire the world. He restored, for many, faith in the possibility of the triumph of good over evil, and of civility over self-interest.

In 1992 we created a new political cartoon strip in South Africa, "Madam & Eve". Conjuring up a daily cartoon in a country which has transformed so quickly, has been daunting. But we have come to realise that writing comedy in the most interesting and passionate country in the world, in the most interesting and passionate time of its history, is actually a rare privilege. Living through the Nelson Mandela era continues to be invigorating, not just for us, but for all South Africans.

The three of us have also been fortunate to meet Nelson Mandela a number of times, and to have heard him commend cartoonists, both local and international, for their role in preserving freedom, exposing corruption – and for just letting people laugh. Coming from a man who himself has the most incredible sense of humour – lightning fast, sharp and direct, hearty and sincere, self-deprecating and humble – his kind and thought-provoking words about our craft will continue to inspire cartoonists everywhere. As many cartoons in these pages show, even the most cynical hacks are allowed, sometimes, to be fans.

Harry Dugmore
Stephen Francis
Rico Schacherl
Johannesburg
October 1999

Sponsor's Message

Late in 1999 we were asked together with others to support a party hosted by Nelson Mandela in Postmasburg, a remote mining and farming town in South Africa's Northern Cape province, as part of the Nelson Mandela Celebration of Children. Thousands of children came from all over this desert territory for the great occasion. Famous people flew in from far continents to join the fun. Madiba as always greeted hundreds of adults and children personally, danced in front of a childrens' choir and brought tears and involuntary broad grins of delight to all who saw him and heard him. This was a great day for the small faraway community: the day the great Madiba, who led South Africa into the light, brought his joy and magic to town and made everyone feel more worthy, important and capable of greater things.

Later on the same day, ten miles away, Associated Manganese mines hosted a Safety Festival with competitions for many mines in the region at its Beeshoek iron ore operation. Standing watching the prize giving with the Chief Executive of the Nelson Mandela Childrens' Fund, we looked down at our feet and saw a small white boy and a slightly older black girl playing gleefully under the benign gaze of their parents amongst the very mixed and happy crowd. Our eyes met and we didn't need to speak our thoughts: those who knew this community only ten years ago with all its segregation, rigidity and fear can appreciate the miracle that has occurred in South Africa over such a short time under the inspired leadership of Nelson Mandela.

Our country has been transformed and a grim destiny has turned into a future full of promise. The most hectic and challenging years of this transformation have been its middle chapters – the nearly ten years from Nelson Mandela's release from prison in February 1990 until his gracious retirement at the inauguration of his elected successor President Thabo Mbeki in June 1999. For South Africans this will always be the Era of Nelson Mandela.

The period of transition from Apartheid to democracy has been hugely problematic. It appeared that things could have fallen apart and gone dreadfully wrong at several key junctures. For millions of South Africans living their lives day to day it has been therefore a time of great uncertainty and anxiety. Above all this turmoil stood Madiba: steadfast, clear in his values and certain of purpose, always seeking the path of reconciliation and mutual respect, daily wielding his well-earned moral stature in a canny way to recruit people from all backgrounds to serve the great mission of the party to which he has remained unswervingly loyal. His gift for symbolic gestures and robust good humour inspired a whole nation to rise above fear and anger. He helped those of us in business as well, as people in all walks of life, to define new roles and purpose. Under his leadership we triumphed and amazed the world.

There have been countless heroes in South Africa who have worked for freedom, democracy and development. There are many at work today. As a great leader, Nelson Mandela has provided both a sure compass for their collective efforts and a sense of urgency and importance to each individual's contribution. The grandfather of 23 constantly reminds all of us with both his words and his actions that the work is for the children, to whom we owe everything.

This wonderful human epic that has touched the lives of so many with inspiration, compassion and humour is captured beautifully through the medium of the cartoonist. The great cartoonists whose work fills this book highlight the essence of the story of Nelson Mandela's life so far. We are proud to be associated with this venture and proud to be South Africans who lived and worked during the Era of Nelson Mandela.

Rick Menell
Anglovaal Mining Limited
October 1999

Chapter 1

The crucible of apartheid

Nelson Mandela was born in 1918, just a few months before the carnage of World War One ended. The "war to end all wars" cost 10 million lives but did little to kill off the primary ideologies of the era: nationalism, racism and an almost universal sexism. Despite the ruin of Europe, the belief that some people – women, Jews, blacks, Asians in particular – were inherently inferior to others took on new and often more violent forms. Democracy was everywhere in its infancy, with old feudal structures of kings and queens as vigorous in Europe as they were in Africa. The European powers had divided Africa among themselves in the 19th century, and they ruled their colonies with variations of iron-handed governance. No-where in the Africa in which Mandela was born did any black African have the vote. And nowhere in the Africa of 1918 did any women have political rights; even white South African women were denied the franchise until 1930.

In the light of where the world stood when Nelson Mandela was born, his – and South Africa's achievements – by the century's end are even more remarkable. In the South Africa of 1918, whites generally agreed that blacks were inferior to whites. But two rather different strands of racial thinking competed for supremacy among the white rulers of the country. There were those who believed that black South Africans were essentially like children who could, with careful nurturing, one day "grow up" and eventually be given "civilised rights". Opposed to this view was that of other whites who believed that black Africans were inherently and permanently inferior. They could thus never be "raised" to the level of the white master race.

In the Second World War those who believed in the former fought against and triumphed over those who believed the latter. The core ideas behind the Thousand Year Reich of Hitler's Herrenvolk and the zealous racism of Hirohito's Japan – the innate superiority of a particular gene pool – were crushed by 1945. Most of the world got the message: within twenty years the European powers had given independence to the majority of their colonies.

OBSESSED WITH RACE

But South Africa would become a major exception to the new colonial consensus. The National Party won control of the South African government in a whites-only general election 1948. Many Nationalists had been ardent Nazi supporters. They were steeped in the belief that blacks were genetically inferior to whites, and that the white "race" would be compromised and its "purity" diluted by contact with blacks. Almost the first laws the National Party Government passed were the Prohibition of Mixed Marriages Act and the Immorality Act. Indeed, until the 1980s it would be a serious crime for black and white to have any kind of sexual relationship. In 1950, just two years after their election, the National Party also passed the Population Registration Act, which categorised all South Africans into rigorously defined ethnic groups.

But in the wake of the defeat of Nazi Germany and its allies, the idea of the genetic racial inferiority of some groups was becoming an anathema. By the time Nelson Mandela was in his twenties, it was becoming unacceptable to deprive blacks of land and political rights on the grounds that blacks were inferior. Coming to power in 1948 on a hard-line racist platform, promising to put "kaffirs in their place", even the Nationalists knew they would soon need a new story, a new ideology and a new grand plan.

THE CREATION OF APARTHEID

For the founders of apartheid, the solution was simple, and, so they believed, even elegant. During the 1950s, partly in response to the successful defiance campaign against racist laws led by Nelson Mandela in 1952, and partly in the face of African nationalism's successes in the rest of Africa (Ghana becoming the first independent African country in 1957), the National Party began to switch tack and embrace the more paternalistic racism which was favoured by Britain, and indeed by most English-speaking white South Africans. The South African Prime Minister, Hendrik Verwoerd, who took power in 1958, started to espouse the view that black people could in fact "grow up", and one day enjoy "adult" political rights. But there was a new and ingenious twist to this story – of course blacks could enjoy political rights – but not in South Africa. Rather create ten tribal "homelands" for all South Africa's black groups, send the Indian population back to India and consider a possible homeland for coloureds as well.

This, in essence, was Verwoerd's dream, and the ideological bedrock of what the world came to know as apartheid. This is what the ANC and Nelson Mandela were up against. Every black South African would be allocated to a "country" where they could enjoy full political rights in time – and a vote, a nationality, a flag, and a separate national anthem. Of course the citizens of these new countries could visit white South Africa – to work in the factories, mines and homes. But they had to go back to their homelands to vote and, when their usefulness to the economy was over, to die. In this vision there would eventually be, in Connie Mulder's famous words in 1978, "no black South Africans".

For white South Africa this new system had the additional benefit of creating a small black middle class working safely within the system. Each homeland would need governments, bureaucrats and officials who would have a deep material stake in preserving the system. Indeed, Mandela's closest childhood friend and relative, KD Matanzima, was an early and ardent supporter of the homeland system that underpinned apartheid.

Richard Smith

The Apartheid government would forcibly move more than three million South Africans to artificial tribal homelands. Here Piet Koornhof, the most famous minister of "plural relations" (a.k.a. the Department in charge of moving blacks around in the 1970s) speaks the double-talk that he would personally become famous for.

FANTASY AND REALITY

Grand apartheid really was a grand plan. But it was so obviously flawed that it is hard to believe that even its adherents really bought into it. Firstly, the apartheid government, following previous white minority governments, proposed giving Africans, already 87% of the population of South Africa, only 13% of the land for the ten independent homelands. In addition, the reality of the South African landscape was that millions of black South Africans resided outside the proposed areas, and would have to be removed to their appropriate ethnic homeland. To make the entire plan even more implausible, millions of black South Africans had also left their rural lands forever and were, by 1948, living in the major cities of South Africa. These second and third-generation urbanites would also have to be removed, if possible. But if this were not possible, the existing black areas of the city would be declared something akin to large "temporary holding areas". There blacks could, by permit, reside for most of the year so as to work in the white-owned factories, mines and homes.

SPARE NO EXPENSE

As contrived as these plans were, the National Party government set about trying to achieve them with a rare sense of divine mission and drive. Nelson Mandela, the ANC and other opposition groups seriously underestimated the determination of National Party zealots to make the unworkable work. By 1975, all ten ethnic homelands had been established, and millions of Africans had been forcibly removed from all over South Africa to what were deemed to be their homelands. Billions of rands were spent creating national capitals, sumptuous airports and other trappings of independence for these new countries.

We easily forget how complex, how crazy and how cruel the racism of apartheid was. The cartoons in this first chapter try to provide a sense of context, a backdrop for what Nelson Mandela and the ANC were up against. Much of it will be familiar to older South Africans, but for younger generations, and for readers less familiar with our history, the absurdity of apartheid bears a brief retelling. This is the context which caused Nelson Mandela to choose the path of liberator-in-chief. As he wrote in his autobiography, *Long Walk to Freedom*:

> "I cannot pinpoint a moment when I became politicized, when I knew that I would spend my life in the liberation struggle. I had no epiphany, no singular revelation, no moment of truth, but a steady accumulation of a thousand slights, and a thousand indignities produced in me an anger, a desire to fight the system that imprisoned my people."

Nelson Mandela would both fight and defeat this system, doing more than any other person to liberate South Africa from the inhumanity of apartheid. ෨෨

This is a homeland

(actual size)

BOPHUTHATSWANA

This is a fragmented homeland

This is a fragmented citizen of a fragmented homeland

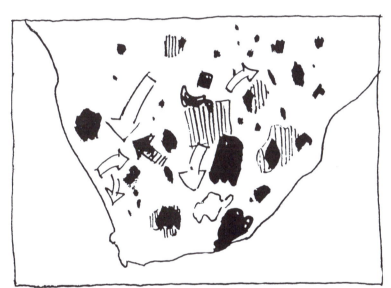

— and this, a fragmented country with fragmented homelands whose fragmented citizens develop separately in their own fragmented way....

Abe Berry, 1970

Not only did the apartheid government allocate only 13% of South Africa's total land mass for black South Africa's "homelands", the reality of the country's geography was such that only the Transkei and Ciskei homelands were in one solid geographical piece. Bophuthatswana for instance was made up of eleven separate pieces of land.

J.H. Jackson, 1959

The world, and South Africa's black population, were not fooled by the pretensions of the proposed homelands system. Mandela writes in his autobiography: "The Bantustan system had been conceived by Dr. H.F. Verwoerd, the Minister of Native Affairs, as a way of muting international criticism of South African racial policies but at the same time institutionalizing apartheid. The idea was to preserve the status quo where three million whites owned 87 per cent of the land, and relegate the eight million Africans to the remaining 13 per cent."

Richard Wilson, 1971

Grand Apartheid was ultimately based on a division of land – an extremely unfair division at that. As Mandela recalled in his autobiography: "The government's intention in creating the homeland system was to keep the Transkei – and other African areas – as reservoirs of cheap labour for white industry. At the same time, the covert goal of the goverment was to create an African middle class to blunt the appeal of the ANC and the liberation struggle."

Plantu, 1985

Gold mining has long been the mainstay of the South African economy. Leaving his rural home in the Transkei, partly to escape an arranged marriage, Mandela arrived in Johannesburg in 1941. He secured a job as a mine security officer at the Crown Mines on the outskirts of Johannesburg. He recalls in his autobiography:

"Gold mining on the Witwatersrand was costly because the ore was low grade and deep under the earth. Only cheap labour in the form of thousands of Africans working long hours for little pay made gold-mining profitable for the mining houses."

BERRY

Abe Berry, 1966

So-called "petty apartheid" (named to distinguish it from "grand apartheid", which referred to the creation of separate tribal homelands) forbade different ethnic groups to share facilities. The Separate Amenities Act ensured that all South Africa's public spaces were segregated, which meant physically dividing parks, beaches and other amenities into different sections. White South Africans relied heavily on domestic workers to bring up their children – and, as Berry depicts in this cartoon, these caregivers had to take their charges to segregated facilities every day.

J. H. Jackson, 1958

By the end of the 1950s the apartheid government had passed legislation to restrict and control every aspect of black life. Mandela writes in his autobiography: "If we had any hopes or illusions about the National Party before they came into office, we were disabused of them quickly. Their threat to put the kaffir in his place was not an idle one." Here Henrick Verwoerd draws the curtain on the limited human rights South Africans experienced in the 1950s.

Bob Connolly, 1960

In the early part of 1960, the ANC made a last attempt to convince the white government that peaceful accommodation of the black majority's political aspirations was possible. The ANC called for an all-inclusive political convention – not unlike the CODESA meetings which eventually took place 31 years later. As Mandela wrote in a letter in 1960: "We have called on the Government to convene an elected National Convention of representatives of all races without delay, and to charge that Convention with the task of drawing up a new Constitution for this country which would be acceptable to all racial groups. We can see no workable alternative to this proposal, except that the Nationalist Government proceeds to enforce a minority decision on all of us, with the certain consequence of still deeper crisis, and a continuing period of strife and disaster ahead. Stated bluntly, the alternatives appear to be these: talk it out, or shoot it out." Verwoerd did not reply to Mandela's prophetic offer. Verwoerd's stature as a hard man, which he no doubt welcomed, became entrenched.

Ashton, 1960

On 21 March 1960, the police at Sharpeville opened fire on a Pan Africanist Congress (PAC) demonstration. The PAC had been formed in 1959 after a small group of "Africanists", who objected to the ANC's co-operation with anti-apartheid-minded whites and Indians, broke away from the ANC and formed their own organisation. Sixty-nine people were shot dead at Sharpeville; most were shot in the back while running away from the police.

Mandela recalled: "The shootings at Sharpeville provoked national turmoil and a government crisis. Outraged protests came in from across the globe, the Johannesburg Stock Exchange plunged, and capital started to flow out of the country. The massacre also precipitated the declaration of a State of Emergency, the banning of the ANC and the PAC, and South Africa's descent into thirty years of outright repression of black political opposition."

David Marais, 1960

By the late 1950s, the apartheid government had made a tactical decision to destroy black resistance to apartheid and to criminalise even mild criticism of apartheid inside the country. The banning of the ANC and PAC in 1960 (the Communist Party had been banned in 1950) signalled the new hard-line attitude that the National Party would become notorious for. Here, Verwoerd and other members of his cabinet drive black opposition groups underground.

Len Sak, 1961

Hardliner B.J. Vorster was made Minister of Justice by Verwoerd in 1961. In a flurry of legislative activity in the early 1960s, the apartheid government swept away the right of habeas corpus, introducing detention without trial, various forms of administrative bannings, house arrests, banishments, and a variety of other repressive measures.

"I must also caution you that anything I may say will be taken down and used as evidence against you."

Graffito (aka Peter Clarke), 1966

As the apartheid government's determination to eradicate all opposition became more apparent, cartoons like this marked the absurdity of the government's claim to respect due legal process.

Scores of anti-apartheid leaders were arrested in the early 1960s, culminating in the mass arrest of the ANC high command in 1963.

"It's not that I'm against democracy – it's just that I've never had much to with it..."

Peter Clarke, 1966

Justice Minister B.J. Vorster was interned during the Second World War for his Nazi sympathies. Vorster became Prime Minister in 1966 following the assassination of Hendrik Verwoerd. Under his ten-year tenure, South Africa would become, for all intents and purposes, a police state.

"No rent... immediate occupation... a life-long lease... the most wonderful view in the world... what more could anyone ask for?"

David Marais, 1966

The eight convicted ANC leaders narrowly escaped the death penalty for treason. Black South Africa was indeed imprisoned. And white South Africans were the jailers. Here B.J. Vorster, then Minister of Justice and later to be Prime Minister, gives what became an apartheid government mantra: Blacks in South Africa have never had it so good. What are they complaining about? Wasn't Robben Island the most beautiful prison you'd ever seen?

Margaret Tabaka, 1964

Nelson Mandela had been arrested in 1962 and sentenced to five years' imprisonment for leaving the country unlawfully. In 1963 almost the entire top leadership of the ANC were arrested at their secret headquarters in Rivonia, and put on trial. Nelson Mandela was brought from prison to join them as "Accused number one".

Mandela's famous four-hour speech from the dock at the conclusion of what became known as the Rivonia Trial would be the last time he was heard in public for 26 years. His closing words to the court have now become the most quoted of all his statements:

"I have fought against white domination, and I have fought against black domination. I have cherished the ideal of a democratic and free society in which all persons live together in harmony and with equal opportunities. It is an ideal which I hope to live for and to achieve. But if needs be, it is an ideal for which I am prepared to die."

Chapter 2

The long, lonely wasted years

The strategy of clamping down hard on the opposition seemed to have paid off for the apartheid government. By 1965 Nelson Mandela and the entire top leadership of the ANC were either in jail or in exile. In the relative calm that followed, Western countries, particularly the UK, poured money into South Africa and its economy grew faster than any other country in the world. South African all-white sports teams beat the best in the world in rugby and cricket, giving whites some reassurance of their superiority. These sporting moments were hyped to the hilt by the government and took the sting from the country being thrown out of the Olympic movement in 1964.

By the early 1970s there was almost no visible resistance to apartheid, other than small-scale protests on a few university campuses, and brave appeals to conscience from organisations like the Black Sash. Even the Liberal Party, a largely white party headed by the famous author Alan Paton, was dissolved in 1968.

But beneath the veneer of this seeming calm, all was not well in the apartheid state. While the Nationalists started to forcibly move millions of Africans to the new tribal homelands, or into new urban ghettos like Soweto, pockets of resistance were springing up both at home and abroad. The ANC began winning friends across Africa, Asia and Europe, opening up offices in dozens of countries. Highly motivated ANC cadres began to receive training in guerrilla war in Eastern bloc countries and in African states. The idea of economic sanctions began to be placed on the world's agenda.

THE WIND OF CHANGE

At home, charismatic new black leaders began to emerge, most famously Steve Biko. Biko led black students out of the largely white student organisation, NUSAS, and formed the South African Students Organisation (SASO) in the late 1960s. By 1973 the labour movement also began stirring again, and effective strikes swept Natal. Indeed, the formation of black trade unions, and later of trade union federations like FOSATU and COSATU, marked critical turning points in organised resistance in South Africa. These union bodies gave opponents of apartheid a powerful new weapon – the withdrawal of labour from the largely white-owned economy – to begin pressing the government. While the ANC-led boycotts of the 1950s had been confined to short and sharp actions, the unions held out the promise of long-term, more crippling economic action.

Jeno Dallos

In South Africa's neighbouring states, and across Africa, the wind of change predicted by British Prime Minister Harold Macmillan in 1960 was blowing with unpredicted strength. Botswana, Swaziland, Lesotho, Malawi, Kenya, Tanzania and Zambia all achieved independence by 1970. Angola and Mozambique became independent in 1975, much to the jubilation of black South Africa. Only South Africa, Namibia (then called South West Africa by the occupying South African government) and Ian Smith's Rhodesia held out as bastions of white rule in Africa by 1975.

1976 – YEAR OF FIRE, YEAR OF ASH

In June 1976, simmering tensions in black schools over the imposition of Afrikaans as a medium of instruction boiled over into mass protest. Marches were organised and although they were entirely peaceful, the South African security forces did not hesitate to use lethal force. On 16 June police opened fire on a pupils' march, killing 13-year-old Hector Petersen. This murder and others provoked a furious reaction – within three days Soweto was in full revolt. Other townships across South Africa quickly joined the uprising, and apartheid security forces would shoot dead hundreds of school children, and detain thousands more, before they restored an uneasy calm in September.

1976 was a landmark year in the history of the South African liberation struggle. The independence of the Transkei in 1976 had been an embarrassing failure for the government, as it failed to win recognition from any country in the world. The rapid spread of black resistance in 1976 had frightened the white government, and shocked the world, as images of young children being gunned down by security forces appeared regularly in foreign newspapers and on foreign television. Thousands of pupils abandoned their studies and fled the country to join the guerrilla armies of the liberation movements in exile. As Mandela recalled:

"Suddenly the young people of South Africa were fired with the spirit of protest and rebellion. Students boycotted schools all across the country. My comrades and I were enormously cheered, as there is nothing so encouraging in prison as learning that the people outside are supporting the cause for which you are inside."

BACKLASH

The National Party government was determined to regain control, no matter what the cost. In 1977 it announced that 19 organisations would be banned, and popular black newspapers such as *The World* would be forced to close down. The black consciousness movement, the inspiring philosophy which emphasised black self-reliance and black pride, and which had fuelled the 1976 uprising, was crushed. On 12 September 1977 Steve Biko, the charismatic and popular leader of SASO, was tortured to death by security police. This high-profile murder evoked condemnation and outrage from around the world. Biko was the 24th detainee to die mysteriously at the hands of the security police while under interrogation. At the Truth Commission hearings in the 1990s, the horrendous torture methods used on detainees were partly revealed. The ruthlessness of the security police, who would ultimately torture over a hundred detainees to death, remains one of the great unpunished crimes of the apartheid era.

TOTAL ONSLAUGHT

Outright repression, even that as brutal as it unleashed in 1976-78, could only provide short-term respite. From the days of Verwoerd, the Nationalist government knew that some kind of political accommodation of black aspirations would eventually have to be made. The homelands system was clearly not working. In 1978 B.J. Vorster was replaced as Prime Minister with the more reform-minded regime of

P.W. Botha and his close ally, General Magnus Malan. Realising that some bold step was needed, Botha sent signals to the world that he was ready to offer concessions, and might even free Mandela under certain strict conditions. This was, in 1978, heady stuff.

But it soon became obvious that Botha had no intention of dismantling apartheid, or of tampering with the central tenet of apartheid ideology – that there would eventually be "no black South Africans". Apartheid with a human face was the most that Botha seemed to aspire to.

ISOLATION AND HARD LABOUR

Until the advent of the Botha government in 1978, Nelson Mandela and other political prisoners were confined to Robben Island, and subject to the harshest possible regime. Like other political prisoners, Mandela was initially restricted to one thirty-minute visit every six months and was allowed to write and receive only one letter every six months. These two letters a year were heavily censored. No newspapers or radios were allowed in the prison at all; Mandela would be deprived of news until 1978 when prisoners were finally allowed heavily censored newspapers.

In his autobiography, Mandela recalls many of the cruelties inflicted upon him and his fellow prisoners during his first decade on Robben Island. His recollections of mining lime in the island's lime quarry, which he did for 13 years, give some indication of the daily indignities that the prisoners suffered:

> "The lime quarry looked like an enormous white crater cut into a rocky hillside. Warders with automatic weapons stood on raised platforms watching us. Unarmed warders walked among us, urging us to work harder. Go on! Go on!, they would shout, as if we were oxen. We worked until four, when we carted the lime to the waiting trucks. By the end of the day, our faces and bodies were caked with white dust."

Confined to the island, and placed in a cell which measured 6 feet by 8 feet, Mandela has referred to this time in prison as "the long, lonely and wasted years". In addition to the privations of prison life, he also had to endure the repeated incarceration of his wife Winnie. In 1969 Winnie was detained without trial and, in Mandela's words, "placed in solitary confinement in Pretoria, denied bail and visitors and relentlessly and brutally interrogated". This systematic torture of his wife – which prison authorities made sure that Mandela heard about – was the cruellest punishment inflicted on Mandela by the authorities. "Nothing", he wrote later, "tested my inner equilibrium as much as the time that Winnie was in solitary confinement."

During the late 1960s both Mandela's mother and his eldest son died. Mandela was refused permission to attend either funeral.

It is one of the great paradoxes of history that all the isolation, the mental and physical torture, and the hard labour seemed only to strengthen Mandela and his comrades. Robben Island became the university of the new South Africa, where hundreds of prisoners discussed ideas, educated and supported each other, took degrees by correspondence and prepared themselves for the day they would be free, and able to release the country from the tyranny of apartheid. With his colleagues, Mandela had the time – 10 000 days in prison – to contemplate the deepest questions of life, and to find their deepest purpose on this earth. Mandela recalled:

> "I seem to arrive more firmly at the conclusion that my own life struggle has had meaning only because, dimly and perhaps incoherently, it has sought to achieve the supreme objective of ensuring that each, without regard to race, colour, gender and social status, could have the possibility to reach for the skies." ๑๑

Marco de Angelis, 1970

Between 1964 and 1976 the apartheid government had comprehensively bottled up black opposition. Political activity inside the country became almost non-existent in the face of intense repression. Foreign investment poured in and the economy boomed.

"I think I can say without fear of contradiction..."

David Marais, 1970

After the assassination of Hendrik Verwoerd in 1966, Justice Minister John Vorster took over as Prime Minister. Vorster had already established a reputation as the "hard man" of apartheid.

Under his prime ministership, which lasted until 1978, the South African Police would be transformed into an effective and deadly repressive force.

Richard Smith & Abbott, 1973

By the late 1960s, the student movements, including the National Union of South African Students (NUSAS) and the Steve Biko-led South African Students Organisation (SASO) were the only significant legal opposition to the government. This wry Smith & Abbott strip does not overstate the risks that student leaders, black and white, took in opposing apartheid. Banning orders became a favourite weapon of the government – such orders confined students to their magisterial districts, subjected them to curfews, and forbade them to meet more than one person at a time.

Clay Bennett, 1985

The ANC in exile had begun reorganising and regrouping in the 1960s. By the early 1970s it had started to win significant victories in mobilising world opinion against the apartheid government. The ANC strategy was to isolate apartheid, building on the victories of South Africa's expulsion from the Commonwealth in 1960, and its exclusion from the Olympics in 1964 and 1970. By the early 1970s limited economic boycotts began to be implemented. This sanctions strategy would become much more effective after the 1976 uprising.

Jimmy Margulies, 1986

By the early 1980s many of the world's largest companies had either chosen or been forced to divest from South Africa. Companies like Pepsi-Cola, Apple computers and Kodak all took the moral high ground by refusing to support the apartheid government. An interesting spin-off around the campaign to isolate South Africa economically was that it transformed debates about business ethics around the world.

Richard Smith, 1973

South Africans, black and white, have always been a sports-mad nation. Some commentators have argued that the sports boycotts, particularly those affecting rugby and cricket, were a key factor in making the white ruling class in South Africa feel their isolation very personally from the rest of the world. This cartoon strip refers to some of the attempts by the South African regime to dress up apartheid as a respectable system of government. Of the many Orwellian terms that the state devised from the 1970s onwards to re-describe apartheid, "vertical differentiation" was the most obtuse.

Rico, 1990

The international cultural boycott of South Africa also started to bite in the 1970s. By the 1980s the only artists who would tour South Africa were either relatively obscure or in the twilight of their careers. The SABC and other government propaganda organs would hype up each visit of a celebrity in an attempt to reassure white South Africans that they were not as isolated as they seemed to be. Most audiences for cultural events, including theatre, musical performances and movies, were segregated until the mid-1980s.

Derek Bauer, 1987

In South Africa's schools and universities, the ideas of black consciousness became a powerful organising ideology. Steve Biko, widely regarded as the most impressive leader of his generation, inspired black South Africans to reject the colonial mentality that made blacks see themselves as inferior to whites. This made Biko an extremely dangerous opponent for the apartheid government. In the wake of the 1976 uprisings, a massive clamp-down on political activists was authorised. Tens of thousands of activists were detained, and the phenomena of deaths in detention began occurring with alarming frequency. In September 1977 Steve Biko was detained by the Port Elizabeth security police and severely tortured. Unconscious, he was transferred in the back of a police van to Pretoria, where he died from his injuries.

Chuck Ayers, 1984

In 1984 Bishop Desmond Tutu was awarded the Nobel Peace Prize. The news was announced amid a wave of unprecedented repression that would foreshadow the declaring of a state of emergency. This great honour for Tutu was a clear signal from the world to the apartheid government, and a vindication of Tutu's consistent and vigorous opposition to apartheid.

Jimmy Margulies, 1985

Margulies' wry look at the limited concessions that the new Botha government promised black South Africans puns on the American notion of a "concession" store. In American racial politics, the watermelon is the symbol of a stereotypical and crude view of African Americans and their lifestyle.

Steve Bell, 1984

The uprising of 1976 created a deep crisis for the ruling National Party. It had become clear that the hard-line approach of the Vorster era was unsustainable. Reform-minded cabinet minister P.W. Botha engineered a palace coup and became Prime Minister in 1978. Botha styled himself as a radical reformer and set about trying to devise a system which would diffuse black political aspirations and ensure the long-term survival of white political power. Steve Bell's cartoon from this era depicts the hearty support that the British Prime Minister Margaret Thatcher gave the Botha government.

Zapiro, 1998

The election and his subsequent inauguration as South Africa's first democratic president have been the crowning achievements of Nelson Mandela's life. They fulfilled a mission that he had felt from a young age. As he recalls in his autobiography: "It was this desire for people to live their lives with dignity and self-respect that animated my life, that transformed a frightened young man into a bold one, that drove a law-abiding attorney to become a criminal, that turned a family-loving husband into a man without a home, that forced a life-loving man to live like a monk. It was during those long and lonely years that my hunger for the freedom of my own people became a hunger for the freedom of all people, black and white. I knew that the oppressor must be liberated just as surely as the oppressed."

Francis, Dugmore & Rico, 1994

Mandela's inauguration speech echoed the words of the great American civil rights leader, Martin Luther King: "Free at last". Even though things had changed dramatically in South Africa, it was clear that certain relationships, particularly economic relationships between white and black, were still going to stay the same, at least for a while.

Zapiro, 1994

The Independent Electoral Commission (IEC) took an inordinate amount of time to count the ballots, and the Commission was still counting until just before Nelson Mandela's inauguration on 10 May. Mandela recalled in his autobiography: "On the day of the inauguration I was overwhelmed with a sense of history. In the first decade of the 20th century, a few years after the bitter Anglo-Boer War, the white-skinned peoples of South Africa patched up their differences and erected a system of racial domination against the dark-skinned peoples of their own land. The structure they created formed the basis of one of the harshest, most inhumane, societies the world has ever known. Now, in the last decade of the 20th century, and my own eighth decade as a man, that system had been overturned forever and replaced by one that recognised the rights and freedom of all peoples regardless of the colours of their skins."

Zapiro, 1994

On Monday 12 May 1994, Nelson Mandela moved into the offices of the presidency in the Union Buildings in Pretoria. Previous white Prime Ministers and Presidents, Hendrik Verwoerd, B.J. Vorster, P.W. Botha and F.W. de Klerk, respond to this situation.

"FORCED REMOVAL"

Findlay, 1994

This cartoon shows F.W. de Klerk and his wife Marike being forced to leave "Libertas", the presidential home, as Nelson Mandela arrives downstairs. The reference to the notorius forced removals of apartheid gives this cartoon its sting.

Grogan, 1991

The ruins of apartheid. It does seem absurd – all the suffering, the twenty to thirty thousand deaths lost directly in the civil war, the millions of stunted lives, the pain of countless families torn apart by the migrant labour system, and the drawn out conflict.

Heng, 1994

Oppressed people throughout the world were inspired by the
1994 election in South Africa and by the end of 300 years of
white minority rule.

Zapiro, 1994

In this moving cartoon, Zapiro chronicles the milestones in Nelson Mandela's life. Mandela was always clear that after the election, hard work lay ahead. As he wrote in his autobiography, "The truth is that we are not yet free; we have merely achieved the freedom to be free, the right not to be oppressed. We have not taken the final step of our journey but the first step on a longer and even more difficult road. For to be free is not merely to cast off one's chains, but to live in a way that respects and enhances the freedom of others. The true test of our devotion to freedom is just beginning."

Chapter 7

The challenges of the rainbow nation

Heng

Reconciliation has been the central theme of Nelson Mandela's presidency. Unlike some of his harder-lined colleagues, Mandela has never underestimated the grievous psychological wounding of apartheid. From the mid-1980s it became clear that of all the obstacles in the way of achieving a democratic South Africa, a full-scale civil war was the most dire and, at points, the most likely. The hatred engendered by the spiral of revenge and retribution, attack and counter-attack in the late 1980s and early 1990s can ruin even prosperous nations. The tragic fiasco of the former Yugoslavia, the self-destruction of Rwanda, the wars between India and Pakistan, the 35 years of non-stop conflict in Angola, all of these point to what South Africa's fate could have been. It was Mandela's determination to seek the road of peace that would lead South Africa away from civil war.

Mandela had four major challenges to deal with:

- neutralising the threat of the white right-wing, and appeasing whites in general who might, as they did in Angola and Mozambique, take fright and flee the country with their much-needed skills and financial capital;

- neutralise and incorporate the ethnic secessionist movement, Inkatha, led by Mangosuthu Buthelezi;

- control and channel the energies of the deeply alienated black township youth whose rage at the inequalities in South Africa and at the humiliations of apartheid knew few boundaries;

- forge a common sense of patriotism and nationhood without which no country has succeeded in the modern era.

This last challenge – getting people to believe in a new imagined identity, and getting them to want to contribute to the creation of a new South Africa – has been the single most testing challenge of Mandela's presidency.

Mandela had already gone a long way to achieving the basis for success in reconciliation in the four years leading up to the 1994 election. His incredible ability to empathise with people from all backgrounds, the ANC's impeccable moral argument, and the support of about 70 per cent of South Africa's population meant that he could command respect from enemies like Constand Viljoen and Mangosuthu Buthelezi. Pulling them both into the

PRISONER, 1963-1990

PRESIDENT, 1994-

Dani Aguila

Zapiro

1994 election and thereby committing them to the rule of law, the parliamentary process, and the rewards of participating in the government – money, recognition, power – owed a great deal to Mandela's personal strategising and diplomatic efforts. Although the contributions of other charismatic negotiators like Cyril Ramaphosa, Thabo Mbeki and Joe Slovo cannot be underestimated, it was primarily Mandela who took the lead in winning over almost every section of white South Africa, from big business to the Afrikaner far-right.

By the time of the Rugby World Cup in 1995, the ANC's and Mandela's reconciliation policy was starting to pay huge dividends. The IFP had been partly pacified by inclusion in the government of national unity. The unpredictable Buthelezi had been largely co-opted and contained in government. Making Buthelezi the Acting President of South Africa when, on occasion, both Mandela and Thabo Mbeki were simultaneously out of the country was a masterstroke of nation-building.

Likewise, Mandela's special attention to the most conservative members of the white community has also paid off handsomely. The images of Mandela having tea with a variety of elderly white former racists, and of bringing them into the fold of the new South Africa, seemed to some to be a waste of presidential time. But breaking bread with the likes of Betsie Verwoerd and Elize Botha (wife of P.W. Botha) was part of a broader campaign to neutralise and allay white fear. By the 1999 election, the National Party and the more right-wing Conservative Party and the Freedom Front saw their election support dwindle into insignificance. The bogey man was gone – and in its place was the friendly and reasonable ANC of Nelson Mandela.

A LOST GENERATION?

Mandela's biggest challenge has been reconciling the more militant younger generations of black South Africans to the reality that economic liberation would be slow in coming. The so-called lost generation, shabbily education by apartheid's demeaning school system, and witness to the raw brutality of a long drawn-out and mostly urban war – have provided acute challenges for the new government. The government under Nelson Mandela has avoided the obvious temptations of wealth redistribution taxes, or the more drastic nationalisation of private white assets. Even land, so systematically stolen from black South Africans for the last hundred years, has been conservatively returned to black owners. White property rights, however illegitimate in certain cases, have been respected.

By 1999 Mandela had achieved many of his reconciliation goals. White hostility to the new South Africa has largely evaporated and white emigration has slowed down. Relations with Inkatha have improved to such an extent that violence in Natal can officially be said to be over. Black South Africans are slowly beginning to see some of the benefits of the government's economic policies, with entrepreneurial opportunities for blacks emerging in every sector of the economy. These may not be the hand-outs that some of Mandela's supporters may have expected but they are the basis for building long-term wealth and prosperity.

A LEGACY WITHOUT LIMITS

Given the challenges of what Mandela faced in 1994, the successes of his first five years of government are extraordinary by just about every measure. South Africa has avoided war and a nascent sense of nationhood is taking root. South Africans on both the right and the left wing of the political spectrum have learned a modicum of respect for each other's views. The economy is poised to begin to deliver tangible benefits to the poorest of the poor. There is much still to achieve, but Mandela has given South Africa a chance to join the pantheon of successful nations. The next five to ten years are going to be critical in determining whether South Africa builds on the start that Mandela's presidency has given us. ೦೨

Makhosini Nyathi, 1994

The challenges faced by Nelson Mandela in his first months of presidency was the subject of many political cartoons. For someone taking over the running of a country with six million unemployed and a legacy of almost forty years of stultifying Bantu education, it was hard even to imagine where one could begin repairing the damage done by apartheid.

Grogan, 1994

Two cartoonists with an entirely different take on the same idea. Tony Grogan shows Mandela as the hero with sleeves rolled up who defeats the giant of apartheid and now has to tackle the relatively minor problem of crime in South Africa.

Zapiro, 1994

Zapiro also sees Mandela in a heroic role as the biblical David. Having now slain the Goliath of apartheid, Mandela has to face up to a much bigger threat – that of criminal violence in South Africa. Zapiro's cartoon has proved to be the more prophetic.

Zapiro, 1994

The ANC was at pains during its election campaign not to allow expectations to soar too high. Nonetheless, South Africa entered its democratic era in a euphoric mood with ordinary people hoping for a rapid rise in their living standards.

Derek Bauer, 1997

Crime would prove to be one of the new government's greatest challenges. Despite high-profile anti-crime initiatives, crime was the one problem that Mandela singularly failed to get to grips with during the course of his presidency. The overall crime rate continued to soar until it stabilised at unacceptably high levels in 1998. This cartoon depicts Mandela lecturing then Minister of Police Sydney Mufamadi and Police Chief George Fivas.

Lou Henning, 1994

Even after the election, sections of the conservative press continued to see Nelson Mandela and the ANC as merely a front for communism. In this cartoon, Ronnie Kasrils, Communist Party stalwart, is whispering to Joe Slovo, leader of the party, with reference to Mandela: "He is not going to make it for long, then you can take over the crown."

In the background, the "ghost" of the Communist Party is waiting in the wings and is also saying, "It's not long now, then I'll take over." Cyril Ramaphosa is depicted as the "second princess" in this particular beauty pageant, and he is shown thinking to himself, "Well, they are both fairly old", a reference to Ramaphosa's supposed ambitions on the presidency. Thabo Mbeki is tying a rope around Ramaphosa's leg. The little bird – a common feature of Lou Henning's cartoons – is asking, "Are these Mr [Kader] Asmal's beauties?" This is a possible reference to his perceived influence of an Indian cabal over the ANC.

Zapiro, 1994

With the taking of high office came unending public scrutiny for Nelson Mandela. South Africa, the world and particularly the South African stock market clung on his every word: the prospects for South Africa's success were seen unfairly to rest on Mandela's shoulders alone. The "Zwelakhe" that Mandela is referring to in this cartoon is Zwelakhe Sisulu, then head of the SABC and son of Nelson Mandela's close friend and fellow ANC stalwart, Walter Sisulu.

Zapiro, 1996

Such was Mandela's perceived influence on the well-being of the country that even the smallest rumour about ill health could cause both local stocks and the South African currency to nose-dive.

The "Parks" that Mandela is talking to in the last caption was his publicity secretary, Parks Mankahlana.

Andy, 1994

One of the most interesting and complex challenges that Mandela faced was the wave of strikes in his first year of office. Workers, particularly government workers, expected a good deal more from the new democratic dispensation than they felt they were receiving.

Zapiro, 1997

Reconciliation was the by-word of Mandela's presidency. Going further than anyone expected him to, Mandela even visited Mrs Betsie Verwoerd, the octogenarian widow of the architect of apartheid, Dr H.F. Verwoerd. She was then living in *Orania*, a prototype whites-only *volkstaat* in one of South Africa's most barren areas. Mrs Verwoerd received Mandela graciously. By 1999 white Afrikaner support for the idea of an independent white homeland had faded into insignificance, partly due to Mandela's efforts to make Afrikaners feel welcome in the new South Africa. The sign in the background reads "whites only" And the coffee mug is engraved with the words "non-white guests".

Zapiro, 1996

Taking the reconciliation theme even further, Mandela became an ardent supporter of the nation's sporting teams. Mandela would drop in on the South African national teams just before a rugby, cricket or soccer game, to give them his best wishes. These encounters appeared to have an electrifying effect on the players. Here the Australian rugby team is represented by a flattened kangaroo: a turbo-charged Springbok team defeated Australia in the opening game of the 1995 Rugby World Cup.

Mandela's support for the almost all-white World Cup rugby team was a tactical masterstroke in terms of bringing about genuine reconciliation in South Africa. Mandela himself, like the rest of the world, was thrilled by the tense on-field encounter. "When it was 12 – 12, I almost collapsed," Mandela recalled. "I was absolutely tense. When I left the stadium (after South Africa's narrow 15 – 12 victory), my nerves were completely shattered."

Zapiro, 1996

Such was Mandela's effect on national sports teams, and their results in matches, a new kind of patriotism began to take hold in South Africa. The South African football team won the Confederation of African States (KAF) cup in 1996, and the national rugby and cricket teams continued to perform above expectations.

Francis, Dugmore & Rico, 1997

Mandela's effect on the sports teams and on ordinary people became known as "Madiba Magic". These cartoons imagine what might have happened had Mandela started believing the popular propaganda about him.

Dr Jack, 1998

The Truth and Reconciliation Commission was one of the boldest initiatives of the Mandela presidency. Although it was always going to be an imperfect process, the TRC has revealed the lengths to which the apartheid government was prepared to go in order to defend their system. Believing the maxim that the truth shall set you free, Mandela supported Archbishop Tutu's drive to reveal the truth about apartheid-era atrocities, without reservation.

Zapiro, 1998

The TRC started its work in 1996. Its brief was straight-forward: uncover the truth about human rights atrocities committed by both the apartheid government and the liberation movements in their struggle against apartheid. The process proved cathartic for South Africa. In Mandela's opinion: "All South Africans face the challenge of coming to terms with the past in ways which will enable us to face the future as a united nation at peace with itself. Ordinary South Africans are determined that the past be known, the better to ensure that it is not repeated."

F. Esterhuyse, 1998

A consequence of the soaring crime rate has been high levels of emigration, particularly by South Africa's white population. Mandela reacted with exasperation to what he perceived as a lack of faith in his leadership, and in South Africa's future. In this cartoon, he says "I can't believe that he is so unpatriotic that he would want to emigrate" -- referring to the barricaded South African citizen. Mandela was unrepentant about his remarks, calling into question the motivations of South Africans who could long endure apartheid, but now felt that the new South Africa had nothing to offer them.

Francis, Dugmore & Rico, 1995

A movie version of Nelson Mandela's life story is in advanced pre-production. Casting is proving to be challenging for the producers, and everyone is hoping that the merchandising strategy, if indeed there is one, will be more tasteful than that depicted here.

Francis, Dugmore & Rico, 1995

Imagine what Hollywood might do to the life story of South
Africa's greatest hero. Maybe the idea of Wesley Snipes playing
Mandela in a movie is not so crazy after all.

Chapter 8

Winnie Mandela

Zapiro

Befitting the Shakespearian hero that many see him as, Mandela's tragic flaw has been, in the eyes of his critics, his relationship with Winnie Madikizela-Mandela. His love for her ran so deep, and his dependence on her during his 27 years in jail was so intense, that a fairytale happy ending seemed inevitable. When Mandela was freed, so the story went, he would lead South Africa to democracy and he and his great love, Winnie, would be President and First Lady. But it was not to be.

LOVE AT FIRST SIGHT

Mandela was already married when he met Winnie in 1957. As he became increasingly committed to the struggle, his marriage to the deeply religious Evelyn fell apart. He was later introduced to Winnie by his friend Oliver Tambo. Mandela remembers: "I cannot say for certain if there is such a thing as love at first sight, but I do know that the moment I first glimpsed Winnie Nonzamo, I knew that I wanted to have her as my wife".

The very next day Nelson contrived to have lunch with her under the pretext of raising money for the Treason Trial. Thus began the forty-year obsession with his beloved and bewitching "Zami".

For Nelson's comrades in the late 1950s, Winnie was young and naïve. Winnie's family were uneasy about Nelson's involvement in the struggle and the fact that he was 16 years her senior. Despite these reservations Winnie and Nelson fell deeply in love and married jubilantly in the Transkei, a year after they had met, on 14 June 1958.

Their initial years together were marked by an intensification of the struggle. Within eighteen months, a state of emergency would be declared, and the ANC banned. Nelson went underground, becoming the renowned "Black Pimpernel". But the effect on his family life was more devastating than even he could have imagined – he dared not go home, knowing he would be arrested. By 1962, he was in jail.

In 1964, a mere six years after they were married, and now with two little girls, Nelson was sentenced to life imprisonment. In his autobiography, *Long Walk to Freedom*, Mandela frequently comments on how his love for Winnie lifted his spirits in his darkest hours and brought him countless moments of comfort. When he was released in 1990 Mandela said he was convinced that the suffering of his wife had been greater than his own. Indeed, in the almost 28 years Mandela was in jail, Winnie remained steadfastly committed to the struggle – and suffered systematic, sustained and brutal persecution by the South African security forces.

ATTACKING NELSON THROUGH WINNIE

Many people have wondered what went wrong. Why did Winnie's life take such ominous turns, which would eventually see her watching her former husband's inauguration from the sidelines, a rather sad and haunted figure?

Many have attempted an explanation for what turned Winnie from "a warm-hearted person into a mad creature", to use the words of Helen Suzman, the liberal lone crusader in

In a largely agricultural area such as that around Reepham in Lincolnshire, the railway offered guaranteed, full-time employment, although as this photograph shows, the work could be as tiring as on local farms. (Author's collection)

until the GNR and MS&LR's Act of Parliament received the Royal Assent in July 1858, sealing an arrangement that had to remain in force for fifty years.

Right from the start, this agreement was beneficial to both companies, and it confirmed the MS&LR and GNR as natural allies against the LNWR, L&YR and MR. But the period of territorial stability in railway politics had not yet emerged, and when a coal rates war broke out in 1871 between the major carriers from the north and Midlands collieries to London, the Great Eastern Railway (GER), operating out of Liverpool Street Station in London, and the L&YR revived an 1864 plan for a new line to connect their two systems. The scheme failed, but sensing an opportunity, Watkin immediately put forward plans for a new line of his own to connect the South Yorkshire Railway (SYR) at Doncaster with the LNWR at Market Harborough on that Company's

branch to Northampton, that in turn was connected to its main line into London. The MS&LR had leased the SYR in 1864 and had been channelling coal from the collieries on that line onto the GNR at Doncaster for its journey south.

Nothing came of Watkin's 'wonderful scheme', but for the Parliamentary session of 1873 he came forward with another joint project, this time in collaboration with the MR. The aim was still to connect Doncaster with Market Harborough, but with the MR instead of the LNWR so that St Pancras and not Euston became the target in London.

Although the joint MR and MS&LR scheme also came to nothing, it is important to note that the MR had already gained much from its liaison with the MS&LR since the demise of the 'Euston Square

Confederacy' at the end of the 1850s. Its trains were able to reach Manchester because the MS&LR had granted it running powers into its side of Manchester London Road Station in 1867. The MR also benefitted from its share of traffic over CLC lines to the west of Manchester, which by the end of the 1870s branched out to Southport, Liverpool, Chester, Northwich and Altrincham. In July 1880, a new and impressive CLC station was opened in Manchester Central (currently that city's GMEX Centre), and within weeks of its opening, the MR diverted its London expresses away from London Road Station into the new terminus.

Ironically it was not until 1892 that the MS&LR was able to run its own trains from the east into Manchester Central Station with the completion of a new connecting line, although it did not completely abandon London Road. That it had taken so long to achieve this new link illustrates not only Watkin's tenacity, but also the fact that he was never a despot: he had to persuade, cajole, and win over his Board to his pet schemes, and all that took time.

In 1879, he had witnessed the GNR come to an accommodation with the GER to satisfy the latter's desire to tap into the South Yorkshire coalfield, by linking up

Manchester, Sheffield & Lincolnshire Railway 2-4-0 No. 314, seen here at Manchester Central at the end of the nineteenth century, had been built at Gorton in 1873. The skies might have been grey, but the engine was polished to a proud, high shine. (Locomotive Publishing Co A2442)

Manchester London Road Station c.1922 with Manchester, Sheffield & Lincolnshire Railway Class 3 2-4-2T No. 599 (built in 1891) approaching the camera. Immediately behind the locomotive and train is the London & North Western Railway (LNWR) section of the Station, with the area used by the MS&LR off to the extreme right. (Stations UK)

and improving various existing lines to form the Great Northern & Great Eastern Joint Railway (GN&GEJR). Much of the route of the GN&GEJR was within a few miles of the course proposed by the GER and L&YR in 1864 and 1871, and it was to the L&YR that Watkin glanced briefly in 1883 when it was suggested the MS&LR could join forces with that Company, and the Metropolitan Railway (MetR), to reach London. Watkin was already Chairman of both the MetR, expanding north out of the heart of London, and the South Eastern Railway (SER), stretching from London Bridge Station in the capital to Dover (amongst other places). It was in this period that Watkin could dream not only of MS&LR trains reaching London, but travelling onwards via these other railways and through a tunnel under the English Channel to France. In 1880 he had become involved in the Submarine Continental Railway, and serious tunnelling did take place, but which, after only two years

work, was abandoned and he then turned his attention to the more realistic, but ultimately fruitless, project of driving a tunnel under the Humber Estuary.

By then, Watkin was in his sixties, and he was becoming more convinced that if he was to see MS&LR trains in London, then he would have to persuade his Company to build its own line to the capital. For most of the 1880s, the benefits for both the MS&LR and GNR of improved Manchester–London services kept this ambition in check, but then at the very end of that decade, with another twenty years of the GNR and MS&LR agreement yet to run, the latter Company made its first tentative southerly move. In July 1889, an Act was passed for an extension from Beighton (just outside Sheffield) to

Emerging from the 1852 bore of the Woodhead Tunnels at Dunford Bridge in about 1925 is one of a number of 2-8-0 locomotives built to John George Robinson's GCR designs by the North British Locomotive Co. of Glasgow at the end of 1917, for use by the military. This particular engine was taken into London & North Eastern Railway stock in 1924 and numbered 6276. (G. Tidey)

The Great Central Railway shared Lincoln Central Station with the Great Northern Railway. In this photograph, taken in about 1923, GCR Class 11B 4-4-0 No.1021 *Queen Mary* waits with an eastbound train. By the time this engine was built in 1902, protection for the driver and fireman had improved since the 1870s. (Author's collection)

The frontage of Liverpool Central Station on Ranelagh Street in the early 1920s. This was the Cheshire Lines Committee's terminus in the city, opened in March 1874, from where the Manchester, Sheffield & Lincolnshire Railway ran some fast, and well-patronised, services to Manchester in direct competition with the LNWR. (Commercial postcard, author's collection)

At the other end of the Cheshire Lines Committee's route from Liverpool and the Wirral was Manchester Central Station, which opened on 1 July 1880, replacing a temporary terminus of 1877. (Grosvenor postcard, author's collection)

a junction with the GNR at Annesley, the tip of that Company's Leen Valley line in the Nottinghamshire coalfield. Ostensibly, the new MS&LR line was to provide better outlets for north Derbyshire collieries, and to get the Company into Nottingham and no further. Within months, however, Watkin wrote to the GNR, outlining why he thought it would be advantageous to both railways if a new line was built from Nottingham to join the MetR outside London, thus creating a new route into the capital. He described the forging of a completely new route as better than 'plastering the old lines', a reference to the additional goods lines that not only the GNR, but the LNWR and MR, had been obliged to lay next to their main-line routes because of increased traffic. Watkin also approached the railway companies already serving Nottingham and Leicester with an offer to allow them access to what could become new 'central' stations.

The responses were inevitable, but it did not prevent the MS&LR applying to Parliament in the 1891 Session for an extension from Annesley through Nottingham, Loughborough, Leicester and Rugby to join the MetR at Aylesbury (that it was to reach in September 1892) and for another line from that Company in the London suburbs into a new terminus close to Boscobel Gardens, Marylebone. Joining in the protests was the Marylebone Cricket Club (MCC), who objected fiercely to the prospect of Lords Cricket Ground being dug up, and also from some very influential Victorian artists living and working in the St John's Wood area. In June 1891, the Bill was defeated, but the Company had invested too much in the project to abandon it and, undeterred, submitted it again, with some modifications, for the next Parliamentary session.

The key to success was to get the GNR to withdraw its objections, so negotiations started immediately in July 1891, headed up by William Pollitt who had become the MS&LR's General Manager in 1886.

By allowing the GNR running powers between Nottingham and Manchester, in exchange for the MS&LR having the same powers on GNR lines west of Doncaster, the GNR's opposition was finally nullified. The continued objections from the MCC and the London artists were not enough to prevent the Bill passing to the formality of a House of Lords hearing and, if it had not been for the premature dissolution of Parliament, the Act would have been secured in 1892. With the completion of the Beighton–Annesley extension, on which MS&LR trains began to run into the GNR's Nottingham London Road Station from 24 October 1892, it had been hoped to continue immediately with the London Extension, but that had to be delayed until the Royal Assent was granted on 28 March 1893.

Watkin was close to achieving his long-held desire to get MS&LR trains into London. He had manoeuvred, negotiated and compromised throughout his career to achieve remarkable things. For him it was entirely appropriate for the Company to change its name from the MS&LR to the Great Central Railway to reflect its new importance. But the fight for a London outlet had been so long, protracted, and waged on so many different fronts, that for many railway experts and economists of the 1890s, there was no longer a need for another north–south main line. Many believed the moment, and Watkin's time, had passed.

A GCR train at Manchester Central Station. The Class 6B 4-4-0, No.424a, was built by the Manchester, Sheffield & Lincolnshire Railway in 1877 and, by the time this photograph was taken, demoted to the 'reserve list' (as indicated by the 'a' suffix). The engine was scrapped in 1919. (W.H. Whitworth/Real Photos)

To London

The 1893 London Extension of the Great Central Railway (GCR) was essentially to be two lines linked to the Metropolitan Railway (MetR). The longest section was to run 92 miles 79 chains (149.65km) from Annesley to a junction with the MetR at Quainton Road, a few miles north of Aylesbury. The shorter section was to branch off from that Company at Canfield Place Junction, Hampstead, just 1 mile 71 chains (3.04km) to a new London terminus at Melcombe Place, Marylebone.

That the two companies were so intimately linked in the London Extension project was due to Watkin's influence as chairman of both companies. Unfortunately, after he resigned from both positions in 1894, relations between the two railways deteriorated rapidly almost to the point of antagonism. One contentious issue was how and where freight to and from destinations south of the Thames was to be handled. Fortunately, the Great Western Railway (GWR) was willing to co-operate with

The enamel station sign at Harrow-on-the-Hill Station in September 1910, under which its joint owners, the Great Central Railway and the Metropolitan Railway, advertise some of their services. (Lens of Sutton Association)

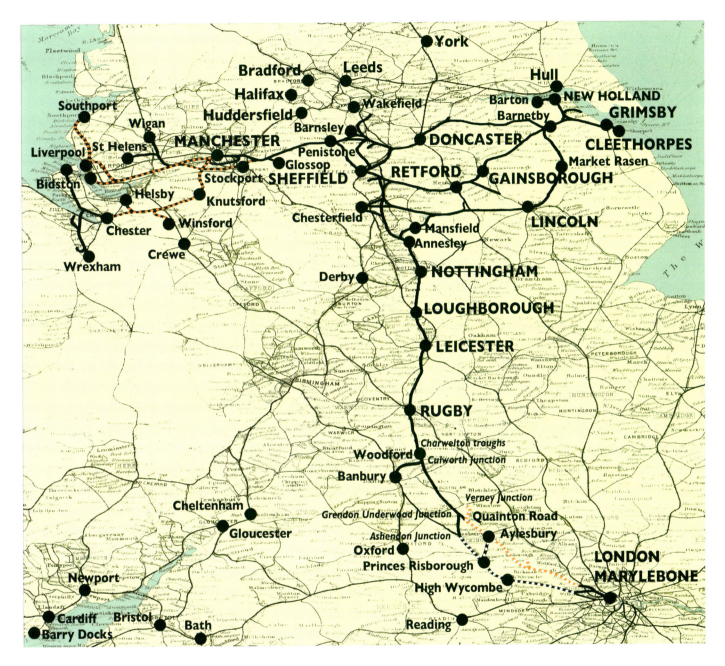

the GCR in this matter and supported the construction of a connection between its main line just north of Banbury to a junction with the GCR just south of Woodford (Culworth Junction).

A little later, in 1898, the GWR also agreed to a joint initiative that would create an alternative approach to the capital for the GCR, avoiding the MetR altogether. By forming a new junction with the GCR at Grendon Underwood just north of Quainton Road, and linking Northolt and Neasden, GCR trains could reach Marylebone via Princes Risborough and High Wycombe. Apart from the Northolt–Neasden, and Grendon Underwood–Ashendon connecting lines, the upgraded route was to be administered by a joint committee of the two railway companies, an Act of Parliament for this being secured on 1 August 1899.

The station sign at Woodford proclaiming it as the 'junction for the Great Western Railway', as well as giving Dover, Folkestone and Stratford-upon-Avon the same billing, indicated how proud the GCR was of its new cross-country connections once the London Extension was completed. (Author's collection)

Section	Opened/First Trains
Annesley to Marylebone	25 July 1898 – goods
Marylebone Passenger Station	9 March 1899 – ceremonial
Annesley (all stations except Nottingham Victoria) to Marylebone Passenger Station	15 March 1899 – passengers
Marylebone Goods Yard	10 April 1899
Nottingham Victoria Station	24 May 1900
Culworth Junction to Banbury (GWR)	1 June 1900 – goods 13 August 1900 – passengers
Harrow-on-the-Hill to Canfield Place Junction (additional up and down lines alongside existing MetR route)	August 1900 (exclusive use by the GCR 31 March 1901)
Grendon Underwood Junction to Ashendon Junction (GCR)	20 November 1905 – goods 2 April 1906 – passengers
Ashendon Junction to Northolt (GW&GCJ Committee)	20 November 1905 – goods 2 April 1906 – passengers
Northolt to Neasden Junction (GCR)	20 November 1905 – goods 2 April 1906 – passengers

Construction of the GCR's new main line was divided between six contractors under the supervision of three engineers – Edward Parry (Annesley to Rugby), and Sir Douglas and Francis Fox (everything else). Engineering a double-track main line through the heart of Nottingham and Leicester, and on the suburban approaches to London, called for ingenuity in design and great care in execution. In Nottingham, for example, 1,300 mainly slum houses were demolished along with a church, schools, workhouse, at least twenty-four public houses and the Guildhall. The northern approaches to both Nottingham and London involved extensive tunnelling; those under Lords Cricket Ground had to be completed, between the playing seasons, during the winter when traditionally no brickwork was attempted. South of Nottingham and at Leicester, long sweeping blue-brick viaducts had to be threaded between existing houses and factories, and riveted steel bridges thrown over other companies' railways, public and private roads, rivers and canals, often at difficult, skew angles.

Despite the considerable challenges, the highest quality of work was achieved in the finish of earthworks, brickwork, track and signalling. Everything on the

A Steam Navvy working at the site of Nottingham Victoria Station c.1897. In the background are the 1887 buildings of the Nottingham Brewery. (S.W.A. Newton/Record Office for Leicestershire, Leicester and Rutland/Kidderminster Railway Museum 038247)

Bulwell Viaduct, north of Nottingham on the London Extension, was another impressive piece of civil engineering, 420yd (384m) long and made up of twenty-six blue-brick arches. It was demolished in 1989. (P.J. Lynch/Kidderminster Railway Museum 094432)

The permanent crossing of the Trent at Wilford consisted of two parallel, double-track bridges of three spans each, built in anticipation of future traffic growth over the London Extension that never materialised. The bridges were dismantled in 1985. (*John Marshall/Kidderminster Railway Museum 069842*)

new line was generous, but not lavish. Apart from on the Marylebone–Canfield Place section, the gradients did not exceed 1 in 176 and there were no awkward track layouts that demanded speed restrictions. The double-track junctions with the GNR north of Nottingham, as well as those on the Great Western & Great Central Joint Committee (GW&GCJ), were installed so that no train had to cross against the flow of traffic, this arrangement often being referred to as a 'flying' junction because one track of the branch line always crossed the main line by a bridge. The GCR's London Extension was designed and laid out to be a fast and efficient railway.

It was not all by design that made the GCR's new railway the most modern main line of its day, however. Many features were the result of the restrictions imposed by the latest Requirements laid down by the Board of Trade for the building of new railways. This explains why there were no road level crossings on the new line. In the 1892 Requirements, No. 29 stated that level crossings on public roads had either to be controlled from a signalbox or by a gate-keeper who had to be provided with a 'lodge' at the crossing. It was, therefore, more economical to build bridges than have to build signalboxes or to employ and house gate-keepers. Advantage was also taken of requirement No.14 that stated, 'Foot-bridges or subways to be provided for passengers to cross the railway at all exchange and other important stations.' Access to almost all the GCR's through passenger stations was via public road bridges. At stations where the road crossed over the railway, a flight of stairs led down from the road to the platforms, whereas at locations where the public road ran beneath the tracks, stairs led upwards to the station. The steps led to

This temporary wooden bridge was erected by contractors Logan & Hemingway to carry materials and workmen across the River Trent at Wilford in the early stages of constructing the Manchester, Sheffield & Lincolnshire Railway's London Extension through Nottingham. (Author's collection)

4-4-0 No.1022 was built in 1902 as one of the Class 11B engines designed to work fast trains over the new London Extension. Trains such as the Manchester Express, seen here near Harrow-on-the-Hill, were made up of new carriages in the latest, but short-lived, livery of French grey over brown, lined out in gold. (Raphael Tuck 'Oilette' postcard – posted 1904)

In the same Class 11B as No.1022, No.1035 was only eight years old when this photograph was taken near Whetstone on 26 March 1910, engine and train racing towards London Marylebone. The engine continued in revenue-earning service until 1949. (Ken Nunn Collection: Locomotive Club of Great Britain)

a central platform, the up line running on one side with the down line on the other thus nullifying the need for a footbridge. The arrangement was more convenient for passengers and meant only one set of platform buildings was required. It also allowed for extra goods lines to be laid on either side if required without disruption to traffic. Only at Carrington and Arkwright Street stations, both on the immediate approaches to the centre of Nottingham, was the conventional arrangement adopted of having two separate platforms either side of the running lines.

At as many stations as possible, the GCR used a standard set of platform buildings. Only at the previously mentioned Nottingham suburban stations, and at Nottingham itself, Loughborough, Leicester and London Marylebone, were the platform buildings unique to those locations.

At Nottingham, the Great Northern Railway (GNR) had eventually accepted the GCR's offer to build and run a joint central station. The result was the most impressive station on the whole London Extension. A two-storey building (with some attic accommodation) 250ft (76.2m) in length, containing booking and other administrative offices with a central clock tower, was erected slightly set back from the public highway to accommodate a forecourt. Behind this building, a huge crater had to be excavated mostly out of solid rock in order to accommodate two, long island platforms each with two blocks of two-storey buildings containing refreshment, dining and tea rooms with attached kitchens, waiting rooms, lavatories and numerous offices. Passenger access to the platforms was via generous staircases branching off from a wide central walkway. Beneath the platforms, and connected to them by hydraulic lifts, were passageways to enable luggage, parcels, newspapers and mail to be moved around without interfering with the platforms. Covering

all but the extremities of those platforms that had their own canopies was a huge overall roof comprising three pitched and glazed roofs supported on riveted-steel columns. The central of the three pitches was the largest, with a span of 84ft (25.6m). So deep below street level were the platforms that only the tops of the 40ft (12.2m) high overall roofs were visible from outside the station.

Due to the GNR's late involvement in the project, Nottingham Station was the only one not ready for the opening of the line to passengers on 15 March 1899. Its construction and running was administered by a joint committee of GNR and GCR staff, the former referring to it as Nottingham Joint Station, and the latter christening it Nottingham Central. When completion was approaching, the opportunity was taken to schedule the official opening to coincide with Queen Victoria's birthday on 24 May 1900, and by this patriotic timetabling, the Town Clerk's suggestion of naming the station after the monarch neatly solved the differences of nomenclature between the two companies.

Marylebone Station was a two-storey building, with attic rooms protruding out of the pitched roof as a number of gable ends. This contained all the essential passenger facilities from booking office to refreshment rooms as well as meeting rooms and other Company offices. It was 341ft (104m) in length, but was completely dwarfed and lost behind the six-storey tower block that was the Great Central Hotel on Marylebone Road. The four, 950ft (289.5m)-long platforms were covered by an overall roof consisting of three glazed and pitched canopies similar in design to those at Nottingham Victoria. Separating the main red-brick building from the platforms was a 200ft (61m) by 100ft (30.5m) 'promenade' or circulating area covered by another arrangement of ridge and furrow canopies set at right angles to those over the platforms.

The interior of Nottingham Victoria Station was a cavernous place with four through platforms and with two twin-track bay platforms at either end. This commercial postcard taken shortly after the station opened clearly captures the size of the space beneath the central overall roofs. (Commercial postcard, author's collection)

Nottingham Victoria Station was designed by local architect Albert Edward Lambert in a neo-Flemish style that was very popular at the time, Marylebone Station incorporating similar elements. Lambert used many of the same architectural features again in his design for the Midland Railway's rival station in Nottingham, rebuilt barely five years after Victoria was finished. (Commercial postcard, author's collection)

Of the other key stations on the GCR's London Extension, Leicester was functional, Loughborough compared well to its Midland Railway (MR) rival in that town, but Rugby was disappointing. At Leicester Station, the length of the one central platform as good as matched those at Nottingham, but unlike that Station, and the recently rebuilt rival MR Leicester Station (1892–4), weather protection was provided by ridge and furrow, glazed canopies and not an overall roof. The platform was raised up on a huge raft above street level and accessed via subways from the booking office on the adjacent Great Central Street. These buildings were considerably more modest than those at Nottingham, reflecting the fact that the GNR had decided against re-routing its existing Leicester branch into the new Station.

More modest again was the Station provided at Loughborough. There the booking offices were located on a road over-bridge – the road predictably christened Great Central Road. Unlike the smaller town and village stations, extra platform buildings were provided at Loughborough, all but the gents' toilets protected from inclement weather by continuous glazed canopies on both sides of the platform of the same design as used at Leicester.

Whereas the GCR's Nottingham, Leicester and Loughborough stations compared favourably with those of their rivals in those places, that built at Rugby was completely out-classed by the LNWR Station serving the town. In 1885 it had been considerably enlarged, and its overall roof rivalled that provided by the GCR at London Marylebone. Apart from the booking office and additional buildings situated on the over-bridge, the GCR's Rugby Station was no larger than any of the other country stations.

Leicester Central Station, of which this was the façade, lacked the grandeur that might have been expected of a city station, the facilities and the architecture being very modest compared with Nottingham Victoria. This was largely because the latter had to handle a wide variety of local as well as national traffic to and from stations on the Great Central Railway as well as the Great Northern Railway, whereas the flow of traffic through Leicester Central Station was less intense. (Commercial WHS postcard, author's collection)

Shining in the sunlight on 15 July 1910, 4-4-2 No. 192 pulls out of Leicester Central at 3.14pm with a Manchester to London Marylebone service. (William Bradshaw/Kidderminster Railway Museum 033105)

An immaculately turned out John George Robinson 4-4-2 No.258, photographed immediately south of Loughborough Central Station. The signalbox on the left was Loughborough South, abolished in the 1920s. (J.A.G.H. Coltas)

The smartly-attired and newly-appointed staff of Brackley Station in Northamptonshire. Behind them, the GCR poster proclaims: 'Rapid Travel in Luxury'. (Author's collection)

The new GCR main line not only catered for passengers, but also for freight traffic. Most stations had modest goods yards with a brick-built shed capable of enlargement if necessary, but more extensive facilities were provided at Nottingham, Leicester and Marylebone. Major new marshalling yards were also laid out at Annesley – mainly for dealing with coal traffic – and Woodford, the latter just north of the junction to Banbury and dealing with all manner of cross-country freight. Together with its new locomotive depot, Woodford immediately required a large number of staff, and much new housing was built by the GCR. Locomotive depots were also built at Annesley, Nottingham, Leicester and Neasden.

In every aspect, the GCR London Extension was a fine railway, but the final expenditure was far in excess of the initial cost estimates. In 1894 the seven contracts were let for £3,182,155 (the equivalent of £311m in 2012 using the retail price index). By the time of its completion the actual cost, taking into account what had to be paid out in compensation and for resettling those displaced when properties were demolished in Nottingham, Leicester and London, was closer to £12m (equating to £1,170m in 2012).

Sir Edward Watkin lived just long enough to realise his dream of MS&LR trains running into a London terminus. He died on 13 April 1901 aged 81, an event that symbolically brought the great Victorian railway age to an end.

The conveyance of coal from South Yorkshire to London was as vital to the financial health of the Great Central Railway as it had been with the Manchester, Sheffield & Lincolnshire Railway. Here 0-6-0 No.985, one of the first batch of 174 Class 9J engines built between 1901 and 1910, works hard through Northwood, fourteen miles from the capital, on the Metropolitan & Great Central Joint Committee line. (Locomotive & General Railway Publishing)

This 0-8-0 No. 957, photographed passing northwards through Nottingham Victoria with a goods train on 14 July 1911, was one of sixteen Class 8A built the previous year. In the building behind the engine, power was generated to run the hydraulic equipment at the station. (F.H. Gillford: R.K. Blencowe Historic Railway Photos Archive)

When this photograph was taken, the locomotive sheds at Neasden had been operational for barely seven years, but the view shows the grimy reality of working with steam engines. The 4-4-2 engine on the left had been put into traffic in the summer of 1906. (E. Ponteau 124)

A southbound coal train on the Great Western & Great Central Joint Committee (GW&GCJ) line outside Ruislip & Ickenham Station (later renamed West Ruislip) in 1934, hauled by a GCR Class 1B 2-6-4T built during the First World War. The second wagon in the train was carrying coal from Gedling Colliery just to the east of Nottingham. (G. Tidey)

This scene at Charwelton shows the standard design of all the masonry signalboxes on the London Extension equipped by the Railway Signal Co. The siding in the foreground led to iron-ore quarries. (Lens of Sutton Association/ PMA/E)

His successor, Lord Wharncliffe, who had died in May 1899, had been replaced by Alexander Henderson, who, along with Sam Fay who had taken over from Sir William Politt as General Manager in 1902, served the GCR until the end of its independent existence in 1922. Another key player in this period was John George Robinson, who became Locomotive Engineer in 1900, and then assumed control of all mechanical engineering on the Railway in 1902. It was the talents of all these personnel that steered the Company most competently and imaginatively until the Government assumed control during the First World War. The London Extension might not have fared so well if it had not been for the initiatives of Fay, who was knighted for his achievements in 1912, and the ability of Robinson's locomotives to run the Company's very varied train timetable.

The first years in the life of the London Extension were the hardest. The locomotives looked extremely smart in their new and elaborate livery, and the new corridor coaches and on-train catering facilities were some of the most modern of their day. But looks apart, the initial passenger services certainly seemed to support the view held by many railway observers that the whole project had been unnecessary. As mentioned in the last chapter, since 1857 the GNR and MS&LR had run expresses between London Kings Cross and Manchester

John George Robinson 4-4-2 No.192 racing the 8.20am Manchester to Marylebone express through Whetstone on 26 March 1910, epitomising the Great Central Railway in its Edwardian prime. (Ken Nunn Collection: Locomotive Club of Great Britain)

'Atlantic' No.258 again, this time photographed at Neasden South Junction heading for the GW&GCJ route north with the 6.20pm express from Marylebone. This locomotive, christened The *Rt. Hon, Viscount Cross GCB GCSI* after a Company director, was built in 1905, the first of four, four-cylinder, compound engines designed by Robinson. (A.L.P. Reavil)

Another Robinson-designed locomotive was this 4-4-2T No. 47, built in 1904 as a member of the 9K Class. Here it is waiting with a London-bound train at South Harrow Station shortly after it opened in 1906, on the new line between Neasden Junction and Northolt Junction, where it connected to the GW&GCJ line through High Wycombe and Princes Risborough to Ashendon Junction. (Locomotive Publishing Co)

London Road via Retford, where the two companies intersected. By the 1890s, the fastest of these trains completed its journey in 4hr 15min to the satisfaction of passengers and the two companies. When the GCR London Extension opened to passengers in 1899, these services came to an end, and both the GCR and the GNR started to run their own London–Manchester trains. The GCR ran five trains in each direction, all generously provided with first and third class dining cars (carriages). Because the track was brand new, speed had to be modest, and so the journey occupied five hours. Invoking its new running powers over the GCR between Nottingham and Manchester, the GNR put on the same number of its own expresses, all with first and third class restaurant cars, hauled throughout by its own engines running to and from London Kings Cross via Grantham and Nottingham. The fastest of these trains took 4hr 30min to complete

the journey. Not only were the times worse than before, but also because the MR and LNWR had been obliged to run their own London–Manchester services to 4hr 15min schedules to compete with the former joint GNR and MS&LR services, their trains became, by default, the fastest between the two cities. The compensation for the GNR was being able to use its new running powers to access its extensive and expensive new Deansgate goods depot and five-storey warehouse adjacent to Manchester Central Station that opened at the end of 1899.

As soon as the London Extension was fit to run trains at speed, the GCR did its very best to win new passenger and freight business. Competition with the GNR, MR and LNWR remained fierce with only a few minutes separating directly competitive services. When the GCR put on a Nottingham–Manchester service in 1hr 59min, for example, the MR responded by re-routing an existing express to link the two

A southbound train formed of Great Western Railway (GWR) carriages hauled by GCR Class 8B 6093 4-4-2 on Charwelton water trough c.1925. (H. Gordon Tidey)

4-4-0 No. 436 'Sir Berkeley Sheffield', photographed in about 1923 hurrying through Rothley, was one of a successful class of Robinson-designed locomotives introduced in 1913 and named after directors of the railway Company. (Locomotive & General Railway Publishing)

cities in just 1hr 45min. GCR improvements were possible when water troughs were brought into operation at Charwelton in 1903, and, in the summer of that year, a non-stop service between London and Sheffield was put on which was soon able to do the journey in three hours.

Over the next few years, timetables were juggled and further minutes were clipped from journey times, but still the MR, LNWR and, to a diminishing extent, the GNR, continued to compete effectively as these extracts from the April 1910 *Bradshaw's* timetables show.

LONDON	SHEFFIELD		MANCHESTER	
Great Central Railway (GCR)				
8.45am	12.28pm	3hrs 43min	1.37pm	4hrs 52min
10.00am	1.32pm	3hrs 32min		
12.15pm	4.01pm	3hrs 46min		
3.15pm	6.12pm	2hrs 57min	7.29pm	4hrs 14min
4.30pm	8.08pm	3hrs 38min	9.22pm	4hrs 52min
6.20pm	9.34pm	3hrs 14min	11.03pm	4hrs 43min
Midland Railway (MR)				
5.00am (divided at Leicester)			9.52am	4hrs 52min
	8.50am	3hrs 50min		
8.00am (divided at Nottingham)			12.42pm	4hrs 42min
	12.00pm	4hrs		
10.00am			1.40pm	3hrs 40min
10.25am	1.52pm	3hrs 27min		
12.00pm			3.50pm	3hrs 50min
1.30pm	4.35pm	3hrs 5min		
2.30pm			6.25pm	3hrs 55min
3.30pm	6.45pm	3hrs 15min		
4.30pm			8.40pm	4hrs 10min
4.55pm	8.20pm	3hrs 25min		
5.35pm			9.22pm	3hrs 4min
6.00pm	9.10pm	3hrs 10min		
6.30pm			10.35pm	4hrs 5min
8.15pm	11.40pm	3hrs 25min		
Great Northern Railway (GNR)				
7.15am	10.47am	3hrs 32min	12.13pm	4hrs 58min
(by changing to GCR train at Retford)				
12.30pm	4.16pm	3hrs 46min		
(by changing to GCR train at Retford)				
1.40pm	5.14pm	3hrs 34min	6.31pm	4hrs 51min
(by changing to GCR train at Retford)				
6.05pm	9.05pm	3hrs	10.08pm	4hrs 3min
(through train worked by GCR locomotives from Grantham)				

LONDON	MANCHESTER	
London & North Western Railway (LNWR)		
7.10am	12.08pm	4hrs 58min
8.30am	12.30pm	4hrs
10.30am	2.05pm	3hrs 35min
12.10pm	3.50pm	3hrs 40min
12.15pm	4.45pm	4hrs 30min
1.30pm	6.05pm	4hrs 35min
2.40pm	6.25pm	3hrs 45min
4.05pm	8.15pm	4hrs 10min
4.10pm	8.57pm	4hrs 47min
6.05pm	9.35pm	3hrs 30min

Probably the most innovative of all the initiatives tried by the GCR, in order to win custom, was its cross-country passenger services run in conjunction, rather than in competition, with other companies. As early as 1900, through trains were put on from Nottingham and Leicester to Blackpool and Fleetwood, with a Leicester to Southampton service running via the connection with the GWR at Banbury. By joining forces with the North Eastern Railway (NER), London & South Western Railway (LSWR) and GWR in 1902, the GCR was able to run through trains between Newcastle-upon-Tyne and Bournemouth, a service that outlived all those companies and continued until the mid-1960s. In 1903 it became possible to travel without changing trains between Manchester and Deal on the south coast, passengers being able to join the service at Sheffield, Nottingham, Leicester, Banbury, Reading, Folkestone and Dover. It was also possible to sit in a GCR carriage that was detached at one station and then worked forward as part of another train to its final destination. The first of these 'through carriages' were laid on between Halifax, Huddersfield, Leeds and Wakefield to Bath and Bristol, and then others soon followed.

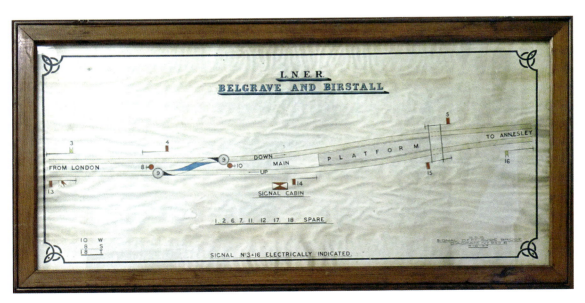

The track diagram from Belgrave & Birstall Signalbox. Originally marked 'G.C.R. Signal Dept. Guide Bridge Diagram No. 959A 4-6-1917', it had been updated sometime after 1923 by the substitution of the initials 'LNER' for the original 'GCR'. (Courtesy Great Central Railway Museum, Loughborough)

In 1912, Robinson designed a new type of express passenger locomotive, the first one named *Sir Sam Fay* after the Company's General Manager, who had been knighted that year. In 1913, five other engines of this class were built, including No. 426 *City of Chester*, seen here at London Marylebone in the early 1920s. The driver is oiling around the two inside cylinders and motion before the engine leaves with its train. (M.W. Earley)

On another day, No. 426 *City of Chester* was photographed in action, pulling the 3.20pm express to Manchester out of Marylebone in 1922. (A.L.P. Reavil)

To improve the efficiency of suburban services out of Marylebone Station, Robinson designed a 4-6-2T engine in 1911, one of the class proudly depicted on this contemporary postcard hauling a train out of London to Aylesbury. (Locomotive Publishing Co. postcard)

Through carriages were a feature of railway operation common to most railway companies in the period immediately before the First World War, as was the provision of 'slip coaches'. This involved detaching a carriage from a train as it passed without stopping through a station. The detached carriage ran under its own momentum into the platform where it was brought to a stand by the guard applying his brake. On the GCR, Penistone, Nottingham, Leicester and Woodford were all served at one time or another by slip coaches.

By 1914, as well as the destinations mentioned above, the GCR was running through services to Barry Docks, Cardiff, Newport, Gloucester, Cheltenham, Darlington, Oxford, Winchester, Hull, Liverpool and Harwich. The ultimate long-distance service appeared just before the GCR was taken over by the LNER, when it became possible – if you had the stamina – to occupy the same carriage from Aberdeen to Penzance. These through services and long-distance trains show just how far relationships between the GCR and other companies had improved since the turn of the century. The prelude to this new period of co-operation had

started in 1901, when, following changes of personnel at both the GCR and the MetR, the relationship between these two companies began to improve. In 1904, following arbitration, it was agreed to transfer to the GCR on a 999-year lease the extra lines the MetR had built for the use of GCR trains between Harrow South Junction and Canfield Place. The remainder of the lines northwards between Harrow South Junction and Quainton Road (including the branch to Verney Junction) were to be administered by a joint committee of the two companies.

The most extreme example of a new *entente cordial* between former rivals, and showing how much had changed in just ten years, came in 1908 when the GCR, GNR and GER agreed to amalgamate. Parliament was not ready to support the amalgamation, however, and after discussions that began to expand into the wider issues of nationalisation, the companies abandoned their bill in 1909.

The London Extension and its services were not the over-riding preoccupation of the GCR in the period between 1900 and its absorption into the LNER in 1923. There were many other concerns that a book of this type does not have the space to examine. There was the Company's marine fleet, new locomotive designs, widening of lines, innovative signalling installations, publicity, new branch lines, labour relations, strikes and other issues too numerous to mention here. Arguably the finest and most significant achievement of the GCR worth singling out, however, was the completion in 1912 of the huge new dock at Immingham. Six years in the making, this was economically far more remunerative than the London Extension, its importance continuing into the twenty-first century, long after the latter had disappeared as a through route.

The Lancashire, Derbyshire & East Coast Railway (LD&ECR) was acquired by the GCR in 1907, this locomotive being an example of one of the thirty-seven engines transferred in the deal. The LD&ECR had opened in 1896 stretching from Chesterfield in Derbyshire, with a branch to within a few miles of Sheffield, to a junction with the Great Northern & Great Eastern Joint Railway just west of Lincoln. It never reached either Lancashire or the East Coast. Passing through an area where new deep coal mines were being sunk, however, did make it a potentially remunerative line, hence the GCR takeover. (Author's collection)

At the very end of the nineteenth century, the GCR, along with the Great Northern Railway and the Midland Railway, needed new locomotives more quickly than they, or any other British contractor, could build them. Consequently, all three companies purchased a number of engines from the USA. The GCR patronised Burnham, Williams & Co. of Philadelphia, whose No. 963, pictured here, was one of twenty engines shipped over in parts during 1900 for assembly at Gorton. (Author's collection)

In 1905 the GCR took over the Wrexham, Mold & Connah's Quay Railway (WM&CQR) and this was one of the locomotives it inherited. It had been built originally as an 0-6-0 for the Manchester & Birmingham Railway in 1846. After that railway became part of the London & North Western Railway, it was rebuilt as a saddle tank and then sold in 1872 to the WM&CQR that had opened six years earlier. The engine was christened *Queen*. In 1880 the wheel arrangement was altered to 0-8-0, then to 0-6-2 in 1888. In 1890 an extensive rebuild was carried out, and finally in 1903 it emerged in the form shown in this photograph. After the WM& CQR was taken over by the GCR, *Queen* became simply No. 400B, remaining active until 1923. (Real Photographs Co.)

To cope with increased traffic to and from the new docks at Immingham (officially opened by HRH King George V on 22 July 1912), the line had to be widened between Wrawby Junction (where the lines from Lincoln, Frodingham and Gainsborough joined) and Brocklesby (where lines diverged to Grimsby and Immingham). As part of the work, three new signalboxes were brought into use at Barnetby, this photograph showing the team completing the connections to Barnetby West in 1916. (Commercial postcard, author's collection)

To Closure

The London & North Eastern Railway (LNER) assumed responsibility for all former Great Central Railway (GCR) lines in 1923, continuing to manage them until British Railways was formed in 1948.

The locally-manufactured Raleigh bicycle in the background of this photograph, taken on 23 June 1923, was undoubtedly how this signalman travelled to the West Platform Signalbox at Nottingham Victoria Station that day. It was only six months since the GCR had become part of the London & North Eastern Railway. (Author's collection)

During those twenty-four years, there were no remarkable events either to enhance or diminish the legacy of the old GCR. Huge quantities of coal were still carried across the network; fish landed at Grimsby still made its way to the industrial centres of the country as well as the capital; passengers could still catch trains to the same destinations as before 1923. Travellers benefitted from new carriages of the same design and quality as used all over the rest of the LNER. From 1936, new steam locomotives of Sir Nigel Gresley's B17 class started to work the principal trains over the London Extension. The LNER ran the trains and maintained the standard of services expected of it, but the pre-First World War spirit of enterprise had gone.

It was the former Great Northern Railway (GNR) main line that captured the limelight. Over that route ran 'The Flying Scotsman' train (sometimes hauled by the locomotive of that same name!), later joined by the record breaking 'Silver Jubilee' and 'Coronation' luxury trains. The streamlined steam locomotives (A4s) that hauled those services were icons of their age, recognised and admired, not just by railway enthusiasts, but also by the wider public. These trains and their engines appeared on the newsreels and in the newspapers, and when one of their

In 1923, W.G.P. Maclure from the GCR became Locomotive Running Superintendent for the Southern Area of the new LNER. One of his first actions was to send a number of GCR engines to work expresses on the former Great Northern Railway main line out of Kings Cross. One of those was Class 9P 4-6-0 No. 1167 *Lloyd George*. The experiment did not last long, and by 29 September 1929, when this photograph was taken at Leicester Central Station, the engine had returned to the GCR main line, stripped of its name and renumbered 6167. (T.G. Hepburn)

Seen here leaving London Marylebone with a local train is brand-new Class 11F 4-4-0 No. 503 *Somme*, named in commemoration of one of the First World War's many terrible battles. It was built only a month before the GCR lost its independence, but by the time it entered traffic, although it sported the GCR's crest underneath its nameplate, the lettering on its tender was L. & N. E. R (London & North Eastern Railway). (Locomotive Publishing Co.)

number – 4468 *Mallard* – captured the world speed record for steam locomotives in July 1938, the whole nation cheered. But there were no 'streamliners' on the old GCR. Two B17s were streamlined to look like A4s in 1937, working on the former Great Eastern Railway (GER) main line out of Liverpool Street, London, but no B17 was so treated for work on the former GCR and there were no record-breaking speed attempts on the line either.

It was as though the old GCR was on autopilot during the 1930s, continuing to do the same tasks it always had without fuss or show. The lack of investment in former GCR lines and services was not a deliberate policy, merely the result of very limited funds being available to maintain the whole of the LNER's network. Major improvements to infrastructure were extremely difficult to finance between the world wars, and despite all the glamour

of the streamliners on the former GNR, the stations, track layouts and signalling on that route remained unaltered throughout LNER ownership, much of it older than its equivalent on the former GCR's London Extension.

The GCR's legacy for running fast passenger trains over that route did continue during the 1930s, but by the end of the decade they were actually slower than services between the same places served by the London, Midland & Scottish Railway (LMS) that had absorbed the former Midland Railway (MR) and London & North Western Railway (LNWR) in 1923. The improvements on LMS lines were due to the introduction of locomotives designed by William Stanier. Just before the outbreak of the Second World War, for example, the LMS was offering eleven expresses between London St Pancras and Nottingham, three

Seen from the road to Woodthorpe village to the south of Loughborough in the mid-1930s, this 1904-built GCR 4-6-0 is heading south with the 'Ports to Ports' service between Newcastle-upon-Tyne, Cardiff and Barry Docks. The service had been initiated by the GCR in 1906 and this photograph shows the set of carriages provided by the Great Western Railway for the train. (Author's collection)

In 1936, fourteen new LNER Class B17 4-6-0s replaced GCR-designed locomotives at Neasden, Leicester and Gorton running sheds. One of those new engines – No. 2851 *Derby County* – is seen here running through Ruddington and heading for London Marylebone shortly before the outbreak of the Second World War. (T.G. Hepburn)

When this photograph was taken at Brackley Station in the 1930s, the former GCR Class 8B 4-4-2, that ten years earlier would have sported an elaborate and colourful livery, was in plain LNER black. The first two carriages in the train were examples of the latest, standard Gresley teak designs. (Lens of Sutton Association)

A scene that illustrates that co-operation between the former GCR and the GWR continued after 1923. LNER Class C1 4-4-2 No. 4434, having come in from the London Extension, stands alongside GWR 2-6-0 No. 4361 at the GWR's Banbury locomotive sheds in the mid-1930s. (L. Hanson)

of those achieving the journey in 2hr 3mins, and none taking more than 2hr 49min. In comparison, the LNER only ran six expresses from London Marylebone to Nottingham Victoria, the two fastest covering the ground in 2hr 16min, the slowest taking 2hr 47min. In the opposite direction, the LMS ran ten expresses, the fastest taking 2hr 3min and the slowest 2hr 55min. The LNER offered six trains from Victoria, the fastest taking 2hr 17min, the slowest 2hr 43min.

The one area where the LNER calculated it could achieve a good return on capital investment in former GCR lines was in improving the movement of freight over the Pennines. Between 1928 and 1931, the two Hattersley Tunnels west of Broadbottom (Mottram) were replaced at some expense by a wide cutting, the work carried out by the same contractor – Logan & Hemingway – that had driven the London Extension through Nottingham. By the time the Hattersley project had been completed, approval had been granted for an extensive new yard between Mottram and Dinting, where freight wagons arriving from the east could be marshalled

prior to working forward to western destinations. Then in 1936, barely a year after that new Mottram Yard became operational, a scheme was approved for the electrification of the main line between Manchester and Sheffield.

Contracts were let and some work was started, including the building of a new electric locomotive. But before any real progress could be made, the Second World War intervened and work stopped. The conflict put an enormous strain on the existing infrastructure, locomotives, stock and particularly railway staff. Between 1939 and 1945, huge quantities of raw materials and all the paraphernalia that maintains a nation in a state of total war were carried on the railways. On the former GCR's London Extension, the yards at Woodford were enlarged and an extensive new rail-connected ordnance depot constructed at Ruddington, just to the south of Nottingham.

After the war, all passenger services throughout the country were slower than in 1939. There was much to be done to revitalise the railways and all the pre-war companies had plans for the future.

LNER Class V2 No. 4773 racing through Wembley Hill on the former Great Western & Great Central Joint Committee route with an excursion a few years after the engine was completed at Doncaster Works at the end of 1936. (Author's collection)

London Marylebone Station in 1938. Built in 1905, the ex-GCR locomotive pictured was destined to work for another ten years before being withdrawn and scrapped. (Author's collection)

This GCR 4-6-0 of 1921, struggling with an east bound coal train on 1 July 1947, dramatically illustrates one of the main reasons why the LNER was keen to electrify the route across the Pennines via the Woodhead Tunnels. The train was passing under Gamesley Bridge that carried the road over the line to Glossop, a structure that had been extensively remodelled in the mid-1930s as part of the work to create Mottram Yard, out of view immediately to the left. (Kemsley Newspapers)

In this photograph taken at the south end of Nottingham Victoria Station on 1 April 1939, everything was grubby, little effort having been made to clean the engines and carriages externally. No. 4588 was built at Doncaster in 1912, originally to work suburban trains in and out of Kings Cross Station for the Great Northern Railway. (J.P. Wilson)

The declaration of war with Germany in September 1939 was only three months away when this photograph was taken on 1 June at Godley Junction. The engine was 4-6-0 No. 5037, an example of the last type of locomotive designed by John George Robinson for the GCR in 1921. (Author's collection)

A rare Second World War photograph of imported USA 2-8-0 Class S160 No. 1846 working a freight train near Quorn & Woodhouse Station on 13 May 1943. (V.R. Webster/Kidderminster Railway Museum 017608)

By the end of the Second World War, all LNER locomotives had been painted black and the Company initials abbreviated as illustrated here on Class B17 No. 2855 *Middlesbrough* passing through Rugby. (A.W.V. Mace: MilePost 92)

Amongst its many new projects, the LNER was keen to restart work on the Woodhead electrification. However, all this planning was being carried out in the face of the imminent nationalisation of the railways, a process that had become inevitable following the landslide victory of the Labour Party in the 1945 General Election. In 1948, British Railways came into being, with all former LNER lines except those in Scotland divided into Eastern and North Eastern Regions, and all former LMS lines except those

In the difficult 1950s, the *Flying Scotsman* locomotive was not as famous as it has become since preservation. Between June 1950 and November 1953 the engine was shedded at Leicester and, during that time, was called upon to work 'The South Yorkshireman', as seen here heading north at Quainton Road Station. (Author's collection)

The east end of Sheffield Victoria Station only a few years after nationalisation, with former LNER Class B1 No. 61248 *Geoffrey Gibbs* on a stopping passenger train. (J.F. Henton)

in Scotland grouped into the London Midland Region. There were subsequent boundary changes, but in essence, old rivalries were perpetuated.

Just before the LNER was wound up, it managed to bestow a name on one of its express services between Sheffield and London Marylebone – *'The Master Cutler'*, followed quickly under new British Railways management by *'The South Yorkshireman'* for a return service between London Marylebone and Bradford.

In reality the move was more symbolic than practical. Hopes for genuine improvements in passenger and freight services over former GCR lines were vested in the electrification project that had survived the transition of the railway network from private to public ownership. In the initial scheme, the existing Woodhead Tunnels were to be retained, but subsequent surveys had shown they were in very poor condition and so the decision had been made to bore a completely new double-track tunnel. This delayed completion of the whole project, the first stage of which was completed in February 1952. The new Woodhead Tunnel was officially opened on 3 June 1954, with the entire route between Manchester and Sheffield turned over to electric traction in January the following year.

On 30 June 1951, one of John George Robinson's 2-8-0s emerges from the single-track Woodhead Tunnel of 1845, the first one to be driven through the Pennines. To the right is the new double-track replacement still three years from completion. (E.R. Morten)

The Manchester, Sheffield & Lincolnshire Railway side of Manchester London Road Station on 18 October 1952 immediately before electrification. To the right, Class A3 No. 60054 *Prince of Wales*, which at the time was a stable mate of *Flying Scotsman* at Leicester, was preparing to leave with the 2.10pm to London Marylebone. (Harold B. Bowtell)

Sheffield Victoria Station photographed in September 1957, the overhead electric power cables a prominent feature of the 'modernised' scene. (Photomatic)

Just two months after this photograph was taken at Fairfield in April 1954, electric traction took over the haulage of all trains between Manchester and Sheffield. Electric multiple units (EMUs) took over local services between Manchester, Hadfield and Glossop, replacing trains such as this one, hauled by No. 67437, a 4-4-2T built in 1905 at Gorton, only a few miles from Fairfield. (Author's collection)

Mottram Viaduct photographed on 2 September 1954 as one of the new electric locomotives crosses with a mixture of old and new coal wagons, and a tank. The stone piers of 1842 originally supported timber arches of the same design used at Dinting. These spans were replaced by box girders in 1860, which were provided with extra support in the form of the two brick piers, seen here, immediately after the First World War. (British Railways (E)

When this photograph was taken on 26 June 1954 at Dinting Station, the passing Manchester–Sheffield express, made up almost entirely of former LNER teak carriages, was being pulled by one of the most up-to-date locomotives in the country, Bo-Bo Class EMI No. 26023, built in 1950. (E.R. Morten)

Magnificent though this achievement was, by the time electric locomotives were effortlessly and smokelessly whisking coal trains through the Pennines, British Railways as a whole was struggling to balance its books. Having seen the Woodhead route transformed, the initial response was for more investment, and in 1955 the Modernisation Plan advocated, amongst other things, the electrification of both the West and East Coast main lines, an extension to the electrified lines in southern England, and the elimination of steam engines, replaced where the lines were not electrified by diesel locomotives. These dreams did not survive a more considered financial analysis, and the East Coast electrification scheme was quickly shelved. But even with revised priorities, the finances of British Railways continued to worsen, requiring new strategies, not for investment, but for rationalisation.

Under LNER management, the GCR's London Extension had to share resources with the former GNR main line. Across the Pennines, the only route the LNER was responsible for was the ex-GCR via Woodhead. In comparison, under British Railways management, the GCR's London Extension was one of four main lines running north from the capital. Connecting the manufacturing centres of Lancashire with their counterparts over the Pennines in Yorkshire, the nationalised railway was having to maintain and operate four routes, three inherited from the LMS.

Competition in the era of private railway companies had been the driver of change, but had led to duplication of routes and services between towns, cities, collieries and ports. One of the main aims of British Railways was to pursue a national strategy that would eradicate duplication. Choice needed to be subjugated to logic. In the 1950s, a passenger still had the choice to travel to Manchester from London Marylebone, London St Pancras or London Euston. But, logically, it was more economical for British Railways to concentrate London–Manchester trains on just one of the routes north out of the capital. As the

The Bournemouth–Newcastle cross-country service passing Leicester South Goods Signalbox on 8 June 1954, the train hauled on that day by former Great Western Railway (GWR) 4-6-0 No. 6979 *Helperley Hall*. (V.R. Webster/Kidderminster Railway Museum 017184)

A southbound train emerging from Mansfield Road Tunnel, Nottingham Victoria, in the early 1950s, a photograph that shows just a little of the huge sandstone crater that had to be excavated sixty years earlier to accommodate the Station. (Author's collection)

An east bound freight train crossing the former Great Northern Railway main line at Retford on 4 September 1953. Both the former GCR and GNR lines at this intersection were controlled from Retford South Signalbox seen on the right. (E.R. Morten)

Throughout the 1950s and into the early 1960s, Nottingham Victoria Station would regularly have to cope with throngs of people catching holiday excursion trains and specials to events such as football matches. The destination of this group of eager travellers in 1961 was not recorded.
(T. Baker: S. Needham collection)

The sign above one of the ticket windows in the booking hall of Nottingham Victoria Station. (Author's collection)

After nationalisation there was very little modernisation carried out on the former GCR's London Extension. At the south end of Leicester Central Station, a couple of colour-light signals replaced semaphores, one of them in the foreground of this photograph taken on 30 August 1952, covered with a hood before it was brought into use. Class B1 No. 61066 passes Leicester South Passenger Signalbox. (V.R. Webster: Kidderminster Railway Museum)

West Coast main line had been chosen for electrification, logic determined Euston was the gateway to Manchester. That meant plans were afoot to withdraw Manchester services from the other London termini. Likewise, British Railways could not justify allowing passengers a choice of four routes across the industrial heartland of the country, between Lancashire and Yorkshire. It was obvious rationalisation would be needed there as well.

When it came to freight, British Railways used the same logic. Coal, so long the stable mineral traffic handled by the country's railways, was still reaching London from the collieries of the north and Midlands via four main lines – the former LNWR and the MR, both run by the LMS between 1923 and 1947, and the former GNR and GCR, both under LNER management in the same period. Following the Clean Air Act of 1956, however, London was consuming far less coal and, consequently, this duplication

of railway infrastructure was obviously not cost effective. Railway photographers might have enjoyed the sight of the fast, 'Windcutter' mineral trains rushing between Annesley and Woodford on the GCR main line, but with a new generation of megawatt electricity power stations planned to come on stream in the 1960s and 1970s, to be served by coal trains running continuously between them and the collieries, the days of the former GCR as a major artery for coal were coming to an end.

In 1958, partly as an outcome of the rational approach to railway management, the former GCR London Extension was transferred from the Eastern Region of British Railways to its London Midland Region. The logic was that the line was geographically and very obviously in London Midland Region territory. It was very much like stating that as trout are fish then it is logical to put them in the ocean with sharks because they are also fish.

The consequence was predictable. The Eastern Region was left with only one main north–south trunk line to deal with, whereas the London Midland Region now had three such routes. As all its limited resources were going towards the electrification and modernisation of the West Coast main line, and as the former MR line to and from St Pancras had already assumed the 'Cinderella role' in the London Midland Region's portfolio, (a situation that continued into the 1980s), the re-allocation of the ex-GCR main line was in reality a death sentence for it.

The retreating Eastern Region took 'The Master Cutler' service with it, and with a touch of historical *deja vu*, because it was still completely within its territory, re-routed the service to and from Kings Cross via Retford! From the beginning of 1960, expresses were withdrawn between London Marylebone and Manchester. After that, only three trains a day plied between London

With only a few months to go before the closure of Charwelton Station in Northamptonshire on 4 March 1963, one of British Railways' standard Class 5 locomotives charges through with a south bound train on recently relaid track. (Milepost MC10055C)

When the London Midland Region of British Railways took over the former GCR London Extension in 1958, its long-term aim might have been to close the line, but it still invested in new signs in its distinctive regional colours for all the stations. (Courtesy GCR Museum, Loughborough)

Before British Railways closed the ex-GCR London Extension as a through route, a number of special enthusiasts' trains were operated. This one pictured at the north end of Nottingham Victoria Station on 13 May 1962 was run by the Railway Correspondence & Travel Society. It had travelled down the East Coast main line to Newark where it had taken the branch to Bottesford and then onwards through Weekday Cross to its final destination. The engine was former Southern Railway 4-4-0 *Cheltenham*, its steam masking its partner, a London, Midland & Scottish Railway 4-4-0, No. 40646. (Author's collection)

and Nottingham, connecting with local services between there and Sheffield. Cross-country services that avoided London altogether continued to operate, it still being possible to travel by train from Sheffield, Nottingham and Leicester to York, Bournemouth, the south coast, Blackpool, Cleethorpes, Scarborough or Swansea and Cardiff. But the run-down of the GCR's London Extension had an unstoppable momentum that only needed the Beeching Report to bring it to an inevitable conclusion.

In 1962 the steam depot at Neasden closed. In March 1963, local services between Aylesbury and Rugby, and between Nottingham and Sheffield, were withdrawn, along with the closure of all the village and small-town stations on the London Extension, with the exception of Brackley, Woodford Halse, Lutterworth, Ashby Magna, East Leake and New Basford. In 1965 all through freight trains

were re-routed away from the line, which enabled the yards and the steam depot at Woodford and Annesley to be closed. The following year, cross-country trains ceased to use the line, and all trains between Aylesbury and Rugby, and north of Nottingham, were withdrawn as from 3 September 1966. As of that date, the GCR's London Extension ceased to be a through route.

Thereafter, and in response to objections to complete closure, diesel multiple units (DMUs) were drafted in to operate a shuttle service between Rugby and Nottingham Victoria. There was pressure to demolish the latter Station quickly because of its city-centre location and redevelop the site as a modern shopping centre, so from 4 September 1967, Arkwright Street was reopened and became the northern terminus of the line from Rugby. Withdrawal of the DMU service had been scheduled for

The special that ran along the London Extension between Sheffield Victoria and London Marylebone on 15 June 1963 was hauled by the recently-restored *Flying Scotsman*, seen bursting out of Sherwood Rise Tunnel north of Nottingham on the return trip. (Author's collection)

British Railways Class 9F 2-10-0 No. 92021 passing northwards through Quorn & Woodhouse Station in 1964, the Station having closed to passengers at the beginning of March the previous year. (Kidderminster Railway Museum 165838)

The Bournemouth–York service sweeping through a dying Loughborough Central Station in April 1966, the goods yard already sold off with new industrial units under construction. (J.A. Evans)

the eighteenth of that month, but further objections forced British Railways to continue to run trains until 3 May 1969.

The GCR's London Extension had lasted as a main line for just seventy years, and to put that into context, if the MR's route between Sheffield, Derby, Nottingham and London St Pancras (the latter having opened in 1868), had closed after seventy years as a through route, that would have occurred in 1938.

No more trains. The remains of the signals at Leicester North with the Central Station in the background, photographed on 20 August 1970. Almost thirty years later the lattice signal bracket seen on the left was to find a new use at Loughborough Central Station. (M.A. King)

Seven months after the last trains ran between Nottingham and Rugby, it was no longer possible to travel over the former GCR main line between Manchester and Sheffield. After considering either the former MR's Hope Valley or the GCR's Woodhead trans-Pennine routes for closure, and in the teeth of determined opposition to both options, British Railways had finally decided to close the latter, and from the beginning of 1970, passenger trains no longer passed through the 1954 Woodhead Tunnel.

On the western side of the Pennines trains plied only between Manchester Piccadilly and Hadfield, and along the branch to Glossop. On the east, Sheffield Victoria Station was closed and passenger services were concentrated on the former MR Station from where trains ran out to join the ex-GCR line to Penistone. But once there, trains only ran to and from Huddersfield along the former Lancashire & Yorkshire Railway (L&YR) branch. For the next eleven years freight traffic continued to use Woodhead Tunnel, but on 17 July 1981 this ended, and when the track was lifted shortly afterwards, it severed a main-line railway link that had been in place for almost 140 years.

Cancels Handbill AD119

Train Service

Nottingham Arkwright Street and Rugby Central.

on and from 1 January 1968 the following service will operate.

					SO			SX
NOTTINGHAM Arkwright St. dep.	07 50	08 22	12 27	13 55	16 17	17 34	18 52
EAST LEAKE ... ... dep.	08 03	08 35	12 40	14 08	16 30	17 47	19 05
LOUGHBOROUGH Central arr.	08 10	08 42	12 47	14 15	16 37	17 54	19 12
" ... dep.	08 11	08 43	12 48	14 16	16 38	17 55	19 13
LEICESTER Central ... ... arr.	08 24	08 56	13 01	14 29	16 51	18 08	19 26
" ... dep.	08 26	08 58	13 03	14 31	16 53	18 10	19 28
ASHBY MAGNA ... ... dep.	08 41	09 13	13 18	14 46	17 08	18 25	19 43
LUTTERWORTH ... ... dep.	08 48	09 20	13 25	14 53	17 15	18 32	19 50
RUGBY Central ... ... arr.	08 57	09 29	13 34	15 02	17 24	18 41	19 59

			SO	SO			SX	
RUGBY Central ... ... dep.	—	07 11	10 30	12 30	15 05	16 20	17 37	18 55
LUTTERWORTH ... ... dep.	—	07 20	10 39	12 39	15 14	16 29	17 46	19 04
ASHBY MAGNA ... ... dep.	—	07 28	10 47	12 47	15 22	16 37	17 54	19 12
LEICESTER Central ... ... arr.	—	07 41	11 00	13 00	15 35	16 50	18 07	19 25
" ... dep.	07 10	07 43	11 02	13 05	15 37	16 55	18 12	19 30
LOUGHBOROUGH Central arr.	07 21	07 54	11 13	13 16	15 48	17 06	18 23	19 41
" ... dep.	07 22	07 55	11 14	13 17	15 49	17 07	18 24	19 42
EAST LEAKE ... ... dep.	07 30	08 03	11 22	13 25	15 57	17 15	18 32	19 50
NOTTINGHAM Arkwright St. arr.	07 42	08 15	11 34	13 37	16 09	17 27	18 44	20 02

Notes: SO—Saturday only.   SX—Saturdays excepted.

This service will provide SECOND CLASS accommodation only.

Passengers will be able to obtain tickets, **between stations served by this Service only,** from the Guard in charge of the train.

Accommodation will be provided for the conveyance of cycles, perambulators, etc., accompanied by passengers, who will be responsible for the removal of these articles from the stations.

Unaccompanied traffic will not be conveyed.

Season tickets, **between stations served by the Service only,** will be issued at Nottingham Midland, Leicester Midland and Rugby Midland Stations.

From:	Notting- ham		East Leake		Lough- boro Cen.		Leicester Central		Ashby Magna		Lutter- worth		Rugby Central	
To:	S	R	S	R	S	R	S	R	S	R	S	R	S	R
Nottingham ...	–	–	2/6	3/9	3/9	5/–	6/3	7/6	8/9	11/–	9/9	13/6	11/9	16/–
East Leake ...	2/6	3/9	–	–	1/4	2/6	4/3	5/6	6/6	10/–	7/9	12/–	9/6	14/6
Loughboro Central	3/9	5/–	1/4	2/6	–	–	2/9	4/6	5/6	9/–	6/3	11/3	8/3	14/3
Leicester Central ...	6/3	7/6	4/3	5/6	2/9	4/6	–	–	2/9	4/9	4/–	6/3	5/6	9/–
Ashby Magna ...	8/9	11/–	6/6	10/–	5/6	9/–	2/9	4/9	–	–	1/2	2/3	3/–	5/6
Lutterworth ...	9/9	13/6	7/9	12/–	6/3	11/3	4/–	6/3	1/2	2/3	–	–	2/–	3/9
Rugby Central ...	11/9	16/–	9/6	14/6	8/3	14/3	5/6	9/–	3/–	5/6	2/–	3/9	–	–

The return fare quoted above is that for Cheap Day Return.

British Rail

London Midland Region

Issued by British Railways
Divisional Manager, Furlong House,
Middle Furlong Road, Nottingham.

AD136   BR 35000   December, 1967

A handbill advertising the diesel multiple unit (DMU) service over the rump of the London Extension. The last train ran on 3 May 1969. (Author's collection)

Preservation

Early Days 1969 – 1976

After the Nottingham–Rugby passenger service was discontinued, the only sections of the Great Central Railway's London Extension that remained attached to the national rail network were between London Marylebone and Harrow-on-the-Hill, used as part of an outer suburban service to Aylesbury, and from Nottingham (Weekday Cross Junction) to the outskirts of Loughborough, to retain rail connections to the Ministry of Defence (MOD) Depot at Ruddington and British Gypsum's Works near East Leake.

Quorn & Woodhouse Station as it appeared in 1970 in the uncertain time between abandonment by British Rail and take over by the preservationists. Fortunately, it did not suffer the same attention from vandals as Belgrave & Birstall Station closer to Leicester. However, the preservationists could not prevent British Rail removing the down line in the summer of 1976, seen here. (Kidderminster Railway Museum)

The fact the last trains ran in 1969 was not significant for British Railways; it was merely the conclusion of a process. For the railway preservation movement, however, the timing was important because it coincided with a period of heighted nostalgia for railways following the implementation of the Beeching Plan of 1963 and the ending of steam traction on Britain's railways in 1968. Those two events had given impetus to a trend that had been growing steadily from the mid-1950s. Since then, volunteers had proved it was not only possible to preserve steam locomotives, but also to run narrow-gauge passenger trains such as those in Wales (Talyllyn Railway in 1951 and Ffestiniog Railway in 1955), and operate standard-gauge, single-track branch lines such as the Bluebell Railway (1960) and the Keighley & Worth Valley Railway (1968). It was only logical, therefore, that the next step should be the acquisition of a double-track main line on which preserved steam locomotives hauling express passenger trains could be run. As soon as the closure of the Great Central Railway's London Extension was announced, it became the obvious candidate, and even before British Railway's last passenger services stopped running, enthusiasts were discussing how they might take over the route.

In January 1969 the Main Line Preservation Group was created, with the aim of acquiring from British Railways the line from Leicester to Nottingham. They earnestly wanted to save everything that remained in situ – buildings, track, signalling, telegraph poles, etc – so they could take over a fully-functional railway. As they had no legal powers, however, they were unable to prevent the removal of equipment. The most notable losses were the signals and signal boxes. (The only signal box that eventually passed into the preservationists' hands *in situ* was at Loughborough, and then that was only as a shell, all the electrical equipment and the lever frame having been removed.) This

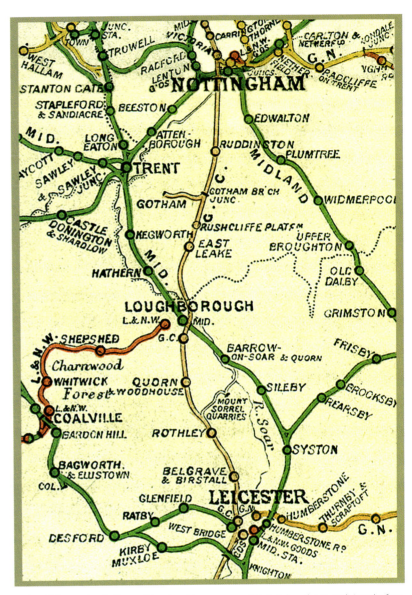

A detail from the Railway Clearing House map of Britain's rail network just before the Grouping of 1923. (Author's collection)

was a crucial period for the Group if it were to prevent further asset stripping.

As discussions and negotiations progressed, the Group's aspirations were refined. The target became the line between Ruddington, just south of the River Trent four miles out of Nottingham, and Abbey Lane Sidings, just north of Leicester Central Station. Then in the spring of 1970 the Group asked British Railways to sell it the line from Loughborough Central Station to Abbey Lane Sidings, although it was still keen to acquire the northern

Some of the Main Line Steam Trust's publicity material of the early 1970s. (Author's collection)

section if sufficient money could be found. At the end of 1971 a charitable trust – the Main Line Steam Trust Ltd – was set up to improve fundraising, by which time the preservationists' focus was on an even shorter section of the line between Loughborough and Thurcaston Road, just south of Belgrave & Birstall Station on the outskirts of Leicester. Unfortunately, as the track was of value to British Railways, it was still being recovered, and the new Trust had little option, but to curtail its ambitions further if it was to stand a chance of acquiring anything on which

it could run trains. By the end of 1972 a purchase price of £383,861 (the equivalent of over £4m in 2012) was agreed for both land and permanent way, the latter being double-track between Loughborough and Quorn & Woodhouse Station, with single-track from there to Belgrave & Birstall Station. In order to keep all this in place, the Trust agreed to pay monthly interest payments of £1,100. In December 1972 Loughborough Station was leased, enthusiasts moving in to undertake basic maintenance, and oversee the delivery of locomotives and rolling stock.

Inevitably, monthly interest payments could not satisfy British Rail indefinitely, and, at the very end of 1975, it announced that unless outright purchase could be concluded by the end of the financial year (ie March 1976), all track and ballast would be recovered. Selling shares in the project seemed the only way to raise the outstanding amount and to facilitate this the Great Central Railway (1976) plc was created. This prompt action and a share issue promised for May 1976 persuaded British Rail to extend its deadline, but despite this, the financial target could still not be reached, and by July only a single line between Loughborough and Quorn & Woodhouse could be purchased. British Rail moved in promptly and during that summer lifted the former down line between those two stations along with the entire remaining track southwards from Rothley to Belgrave & Birstall. Chastened by this action, the Great Central Railway (1976) plc negotiated a large bank loan so that in early 1977 it was able to buy the section from Quorn to Rothley.

That left enthusiasts with just over five miles of single-track between Loughborough and Rothley, and a future of seemingly perpetual bank repayments. For many in 1977, economic realities had abruptly woken them from their dream of a preserved double-track main line.

Creation of a Branch Line 1977 – 1990

The first enthusiast-owned steam-hauled trains on which the public could travel had started to ply between Loughborough Central and Quorn & Woodhouse from 30 September 1973. Three years later services were extended to Rothley Station, and in 1978 the coveted Light Railway Order was granted by the Department of the Environment, ending the requirement that British Rail staff had to supervise all train movements. From then on, trained

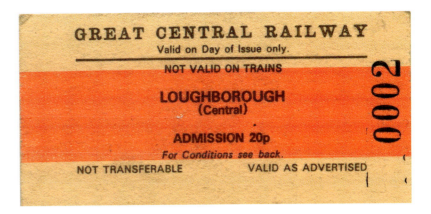

volunteers and staff employed by Great Central Railway (1976) plc ran the trains.

For the next twelve years, the railway's priority was keeping those trains running. In 1973 work had started on erecting a shed at the north end of Loughborough Station in which the restoration and the servicing of locomotives could take place. During the 1980s there were some notable achievements by the railway's own volunteers and by those working for individual locomotive societies.

In 1986 a national milestone in locomotive restoration, a project once deemed foolhardy, was reached when British Railways 4-6-2 No 71000 *Duke of Gloucester* was steamed. At the end of the 1960s, its original three cylinders had been removed for display at the Science Museum, London, so new ones had to be cast and machined, and other vital parts of the valve gear forged and fitted, something thought beyond the resources of 'amateurs'.

During the same period, steady progress was made on restoring passenger carriages and maintaining them in running order. In 1981, Railway Vehicle Preservations Ltd (RVP), which had started in 1968 as the Lea Valley Railway Carriage & Wagon Group, moved to Loughborough, bringing with it its existing collection of historic rolling stock. As well as restoration work, it looked after those already in traffic on the line.

The 1980s were both challenging and exciting times for everyone involved with

The Great Adventure of the
Great Central Railway

Steam trains run throughout the year from Loughborough Central through Quorn and Woodhouse to Rothley. The Great Central Line offers nostalgia, sight seeing and a great day out for all ages, steaming through Leicestershire's hunting country and crossing the picturesque Swithland Reservoir.

1979 publicity.
(Author's collection)

1979 timetable.
(Author's collection)

PASSENGER TIMETABLE

1979

Miles				Wednesdays and Thursdays					Saturdays and Sundays					
				A	A	A	A		X	X			C	D
0	LOUGHBOROUGH CENTRAL	..	.. dep.	2.30	3.45	5.00	7.30	..	11.45	1.15	2.45	4.00	5.15	7.30
2	Quorn & Woodhouse	.. ..	.. arr.	2.38	3.53	5.08	7.38	..	11.53	1.23	2.53	4.08	5.23	..
			dep.	2.40	3.55	5.10	7.40	..	11.55	1.25	2.55	4.10	5.25	..
5	ROTHLEY ..	.. ..	.. arr.	2.51	4.06	5.21	7.51	..	12.06	1.36	3.06	4.21	5.36	8.20

REFRESHMENT FACILITIES ARE AVAILABLE AT LOUGHBOROUGH CENTRAL AND ROTHLEY STATIONS AND A BUFFET CAR SERVING LIGHT REFRESHMENTS AND DRINKS IS INCLUDED ON ALL TRAINS

				A	A	A	A	B	X				C	D
0	ROTHLEY ..	.. ..	.. dep.	3.05	4.20	5.35	8.05	11.00	12.20	1.55	3.20	4.35	5.50	8.40
3	Quorn & Woodhouse	.. ..	.. arr.	3.16	4.31	5.46	8.16	11.11	12.31	2.06	3.31	4.46	6.01	..
			dep.	3.18	4.33	5.48	8.18	11.13	12.32	2.08	3.33	4.48	6.03	..
5	LOUGHBOROUGH CENTRAL	..	.. arr.	3.26	4.41	5.56	8.26	11.21	12.41	2.16	3.41	4.56	6.11	9.00

Booking Offices will close two minutes before the departure of each train.

A–Wednesdays and Thursdays only 4th July to 30th August.   B–Sundays only.
C–Saturdays only from 7th April to 25th August, Sundays only from 8th April to 14th October.
D–Special Dinner Service runs as advertised (advance booking only).   X–Luncheon Service (advance booking only)

Trains will also run on Easter Monday and Tuesday 16th and 17th April, May Day, Spring Bank Holiday 28th and 29th May, August Bank Holiday 27th and 28th August and Boxing Day 26th December.

No services will operate on Good Friday 13th April or Christmas Day 25th December.

A special timetable may operate on public holidays and additional trains may run subject to demand.
The Company reserves the right to deviate from or suspend the above timetable subject to operational considerations.

In 1975 4-4-0 *Butler Henderson*, built in 1919 as the first of its class, and preserved as part of the National Collection, was moved from Clapham Transport Museum to the Main Line Steam Trust. After a period on static display, the engine was put back into working order at Loughborough and steamed in March 1982. Seen here running into Rothley station, it remained on the railway until the spring of 1992 when it was moved to the National Railway Museum in York. (Author)

the preserved railway, its locomotives, carriages and infrastructure. It was a decade when enthusiastic volunteers mastered all manner of skills once thought the preserve of professional railwaymen (many of whom, of course, were volunteers themselves).

It was also a period of perpetual financial worries, with all departments always struggling to control budgets so that the whole operation would remain solvent. Ironically, what also added to these pressures was the general public's growing appetite for all things 'heritage'. Preserved railways, along with new museums and theme parks, all became popular visitor attractions during the 1980s. There was real competition between attractions all around the country, with success being measured in the number of paying visitors. It was no longer enough

to advertise the presence of a preserved section of the old Great Central Railway in Leicestershire, or to appeal just to railway enthusiasts. The focus of advertising changed from what old things you might see during a visit to the 'experience' that would be had and how exciting it could be for all the family. Special events became vital in maintaining interest and to ensure return visits: for example, 'Santa Specials' at Christmas, family-friendly bonfire night and Easter events, and 'Friends of Thomas the Tank Engine' weekends.

It is probably fair to state that during the 1980s the emphasis for the Great Central Railway (1976) plc was on running a visitor attraction rather than on recreating a main-line railway. By the close of the decade the railway had taken on the appearance of a typical single-track, heritage branch line,

This privately-preserved Class B1 4-6-0 arrived at Loughborough in July 1978 in working order, painted in LNER apple-green livery and named *Mayflower* after another member of the class that had been scrapped by British Railways. Like *Butler Henderson* it was a popular performer on the preserved line during the 1980s. (Author)

1979 family ticket.
(Author collection)

Butler Henderson departing from Loughborough Central Station on 29 August 1983. Semaphore signals had been erected by the preservationists but were yet to be brought into use. (Author)

Mayflower pulling into Rothley Station in 1983 when this station was then the end of the line from Loughborough. (Author)

An atmospheric nocturnal view of *Butler Henderson* and ex-Great Western Railway 4-6-0 No. 6990 *Witherslack Hall* outside Loughborough Shed on the evening of 18 November 1989. Bought from British Railways by a group of enthusiasts, *Witherslack Hall* had found a home at Loughborough in 1975. The restoration of steam locomotives was still in its infancy at that time, but the engine did steam again in 1986. (Author's collection)

offering all that was expected of such lines: everything from special events to souvenirs, basic catering and special dining trains. For other than diehard railway enthusiasts, reinstating double-track was viewed as an unremunerated goal that would merely add to operating costs rather than boost income.

Demonstrating they could run a successful heritage business, however, attracted some very useful allies during the 1980s. Once viewed with scepticism or merely tolerated by local authorities, many preservation organisations found themselves being written into leisure and tourism strategies, and this was also true for the Great Central Railway (1976) plc. The first substantial local authority support had come in 1978 when Charnwood Borough Council bought the trackbed between Loughborough and Belgrave & Birstall, and leased it back to the railway.

Within a few years, attention turned to extending the line to the site of Belgrave & Birstall Station. This was partly in response to plans to re-route the A46 around Leicester that would cut across the trackbed on this section of line and might jeopardise any future extension, but also because as part of the station site lay within the boundaries of the City of Leicester, this would allow the railway to benefit from that council's support as well. On 8 July 1985, the 'Birstall Extension Appeal' was launched at Rothley Station by HRH the Duke of Gloucester, and by the end of the year, with the target set at £246,000, almost half that amount had been raised. Charnwood Borough Council allocated £88,000 towards the project and a £133,000 Manpower Services Commission (MSC) project was secured that would enable thirty-one previously unemployed young men to work for a year clearing the track-bed and laying track.

For the next three years, Rothley and Quorn & Woodhouse became the centres of much activity. At the former, as well as

the delivery of materials and equipment for the Birstall extension, the GCR timber signal box from Blind Lane was re-erected adjacent to the down platform, to eventually signal the existing track layout there and access to the Birstall extension. Ground frames were installed at the north and south ends of the station to operate the points there until the signal box was fully commissioned in 1993.

LMS Class 8F 2-8-0 No. 48305 pulling away purposefully from Loughborough on 4 June 1995 with a train for Leicester North. The engine had re-entered service in February that year, after a group of dedicated volunteers had spent ten years restoring it following its rescue from Barry Scrapyard in November 1985. The down home signals and their supporting bracket seen to the left of the engine were taken out of use as part of the double-track project, the bracket being physically removed on 15 May 2000. (Author)

A view looking south from Beeches Road Bridge, Loughborough, on 4 June 1995 with the signal that had been erected almost exactly ten years previously in the background. Built in 1936, LMS 4-6-0 No. 5231 was one of the last steam locomotives to work for British Railways, in 1968. The engine also had the distinction of being one of the first main-line engines to arrive at Loughborough in 1973. In this photograph, the engine was carrying the 'Silver Jubilee' headboard made in 1994 when the railway was celebrating the twenty-fifth anniversary of the Main Line Preservation Group. (Author)

Belgrave & Birstall Station photographed on 16 August 1947 as three-month-old LNER Class B1 No. 1158 passes through with a London-bound express. Almost exactly thirty years later all the station buildings had to be demolished after they had been rendered unsafe by vandals, and the entrance from the bridge to the platform had to be bricked up. (V.R. Webster/Kidderminster Railway Museum 017677)

A brand new shed, 97ft (29.5m) by 64ft (19.5m), for the use of the locomotive department was erected south-east of the Station. Concurrently, plans were unveiled to develop the site of Swithland Sidings as the railway's special events arena instead of the former goods yard at Quorn & Woodhouse Station that had been used for that purpose for many years. A new single platform and 200-place car park would be provided at Swithland so that new sidings could be laid and a carriage shed built at Quorn & Woodhouse.

Attention then turned to improving the operation of trains by completing the long planned for loop there. This was achieved in 1986 and the following year work started on the refurbishment of the former MS&LR signal box from Market Rasen that had been languishing at the site since removal from Lincolnshire in 1981. This was completed by another MSC scheme. Brackets for the new signals to the north and south of the Station to control the loop were erected at the very end of April 1987 by the railway's own personnel, and in the autumn, the MSC team re-installed the lever frame into the signal box. The railway's Signal & Telegraph (S&T) department's attention then turned to designing new locking for the frame and planning for single-line token working between there and Loughborough.

In June 1988 a revamped MSC scheme completed track laying on the Birstall Extension, by which time it had been decided to remove the Belgrave & Birstall Station's island platform and create an impressive new terminus at the far south end of the site. This new building would be the railway's contribution to Leicester City Council's plans to develop a 'Beamish'-style open-air museum adjacent to the line. After three years of hard work, the adrenaline was pumping. But then everything changed.

Spring time at Rothley. The former 1905 GCR signal box from Blind Lane, near Wembley, taken down in 1977, was stored at Loughborough until it could be re-erected at Rothley in 1985. The lamp hut was originally at Whetstone, and after a period serving as a garden shed, was acquired and moved to Rothley in 2009. (Author)

In the space of a few months, the plans of the Great Central Railway (1976) plc were completely recast and all work on existing projects was put on hold. It was almost as though at the very end of the 1980s the management had undergone a religious conversion and had suddenly come to believe that improving the railway's facilities so that it could function more efficiently as a branch line was a false god, and that they had drifted too far from the 1969 path of preserving a double-track main line. The Spring 1990 edition of 'Main-Line' No 68 (the magazine of the MLST and Great Central Railway (1976) plc) broke the news. Double-track would be re-instated between Quorn & Woodhouse and Rothley with long passing loops either side of the line at Swithland Sidings: 'The provision of facilities for double-track operation are considered by the directors to be essential if the Great Central Railway is to fulfil its promise of operating large steam locomotives under realistic conditions.' wrote the Chairman of Great Central (1976) plc.

With the plans to turn Swithland Sidings into the railway's special events arena jettisoned, Quorn & Woodhouse had to regain its former role. This in turn meant the intention to build a new carriage shed and sidings there had to be abandoned, even though the stanchions had been delivered to site. To compensate in some

way for this change in plans, the almost complete locomotive shed at Rothley would be developed for carriage restoration by RVP although it appeared it would have to share the venue with the civil engineering department. The double-track project meant the resignalling at Quorn would also have to be completely revised, so only basic electrical and plumbing work would be completed. (The signal brackets installed in 1987 were uprooted in May 1991 and moved to Rothley.) And finally, it was announced that the grand new terminus at Belgrave & Birstall Station would be christened 'Leicester North'.

Creation of a Main Line 1991 – 2012

The Birstall Extension was officially opened on 15 November 1990 when a special train of dignitaries was run and a plaque unveiled at Rothley by Dame Margaret Weston DBE, then President of the Association of Railway Preservation Societies. Until the end of June the following year, passengers had to change to a 'push and pull' train or DMU at Rothley, because there was no platform or run-round facilities at Leicester North. Then, on 5 July 1991, the new, single-platform station was officially opened by the running of the National Railway Museum's replica *Rocket* and train, with an actor playing the role of Leicester's excursion pioneer, Thomas Cook, and with the Rt. Hon. Michael Heseltine MP as guest of honour. Through services to and from Loughborough began that day.

It was a proud moment for everyone involved, but in some ways, this southern expansion was the culmination of a different management strategy, one that by then had been superseded by a broader vision, that of operating a double-track main line. From something that had been considered in the 1970s as impossible and then viewed in the 1980s as rather an academic goal, running the only preserved

Great Central Railway Loughborough Central–Leicester North return ticket, 1992.

double-track main line in the country was being seen as a very powerful marketing tool that would place the Great Central Railway in a unique position amongst other heritage railways. That this vision had been resurrected in 1990 was due in no small part to the financial commitment of one-time GCR director David Clarke. It was his wish, as a signalman on the former Great Central & Great Western Joint Railway around Northolt during the Second World War, to see Swithland Sidings equipped with an appropriate GCR signal box working Great Western Railway style lower-quadrant semaphores as on the section of line he had worked on.

With his financial input matched by successful fund-raising, overdrafts were reduced and work progressed purposefully throughout the 1990s, double-track by then, planned to extend all the way from Loughborough to Rothley. During November 1990, signalling equipment was recovered from Aylesbury along with the fifty-five-lever GWR frame from Aylesbury South Signal box, the operating room section (the timber top half) of which was removed and delivered to Quorn & Woodhouse in February the following year. In April 1992 it was carefully moved to Swithland Sidings and hoisted onto a new brick base. By the end

On part of the site of Belgrave & Birstall Station, the Great Central Railway plc's Leicester North came into use in November 1990 and was ceremoniously opened on 5 July 1991. The plans for grand buildings there came to nothing and it was another ten years before the modest brick buildings seen here were erected. The canopy was only completed in 2009. This photograph taken on 1 September 2013 shows the first northbound departure of the day. (Author)

of 1993, double-track and the up and down loops were in place there.

Management continued to hold its nerve despite criticism, and between 1996 (when the Company revised its name to 'Great Central Railway plc') and 2000 the track layout at Loughborough was reorganised so that, after completion of resignalling there and at Rothley, double-track operation was brought into use on Sunday, 20 May, a week before the busy 27 – 29 May Bank Holiday. It was a tremendous achievement fully justifying the boldness shown by the directors back in 1990.

Following Clarke's death in July 2002, the David Clarke Railway Trust was set up which eventually merged with the Main Line Steam Trust to act as the Railway's single fund-raising organisation. In 2004 the new signalling arrangement was brought into use at Quorn & Woodhouse and the final milestone in the double-track project was reached when Swithland Sidings Signal-box was 'switched in' on 30 May 2012.

For signalling enthusiasts, this created another feature unique to any preserved railway in this country, namely three consecutive, double-track, absolute block

A photograph taken during a special open day in September 1996 to show the progress that had been made at Swithland Sidings. As well as the signal box and its lever frame, the four running lines were already in situ outside. (Author)

Visiting from the National Railway Museum, former LNER Class V2 2-6-2 *Green Arrow* in its authentic original livery of apple green makes a vigorous start from Loughborough Central in the summer of 2006. (Author)

The working of trains over the reinstated double-track section between Loughborough and Rothley had been in operation barely a week when this photograph was taken on 4 June 2000, showing V2 2-6-2 *Green Arrow* running into Rothley Station from the north. (Author)

Installed during 1998, the metal lattice bracket seen here on the left next to Beeches Road Bridge, Loughborough, was saved from Leicester North after closure, the wooden posts or dolls supporting the semaphores obtained from the preserved Nene Valley Railway. All these signals, including the four shunting signals on the right controlling the various routes into Loughborough Central Station, were installed as part of the double-track project. (Author)

Photographed in early 2001, the different colours of the ballast around the track at the south end of Loughborough Central betray the modifications made as part of the double-track project. Class B1 No. 61264 heads away southwards. (Author)

Completion of double-track between Loughborough and Rothley, with fully signalled loops at Swithland Sidings, improved flexibility in the running of trains, particularly during special events. On 7 February 2016, 0-6-0T No. 47406 heads away from Loughborough with the 'Windcutter'. (Author)

In the 1950s, the fast mineral trains that plied between Annesley and Woodford were nicknamed 'Windcutters', or 'Runners' by the men who had to work them. Following an appeal in 'Steam Railway' in 1992, £14,000 was raised to buy and restore as many surviving British Railways-built 16-ton steel mineral wagons as possible in order to recreate a 'Windcutter' on the preserved Great Central Railway. During the 2016 Spring Gala, such a train was photographed rumbling away from Loughborough. (Author)

The signalling at Quorn & Woodhouse, as part of the double-track project, was commissioned on 17 January 2004. It is a credit to all those who were involved in its planning and implementation. (Author)

Recently returned to traffic after overhaul, 4-6-0 No. 6990 *Witherslack Hall* is pulling away from Quorn & Woodhouse Station on 31 January 2016. When brand new in 1948, this engine was involved in exchange trials carried out by the new British Railways to assess the merits of examples of the 'Big Four' engines on lines they were not designed to work. Built at the Great Western Railway's works at Swindon, *Witherslack Hall* worked the GCR's London Extension in the summer of 1948. (Author)

Part of the up platform at Quorn & Woodhouse Station as it appeared in 2013. At the end of the platform, probably ignored by the majority of visitors, is an ex-LNER mechanical colour-light signal, an example of the attention to historical detail shown by the GCR's Signal & Telegraph (S&T) Department. (Author)

The impressive array of British Railways, Western Region, lower-quadrant semaphore signals at Swithland Sidings. The 2014 RVP carriage sheds are just visible behind the backing signal on the right. (Author)

Swithland Sidings Signalbox, September 2013. (Author)

A view looking north towards Swithland Sidings from the station over-bridge at Rothley in the summer of 2013. British Railways 2-6-0 No. 46521 was another locomotive rescued from Barry Scrapyard. Bought privately and restored between 1971 and 1974 at Bridgnorth on the preserved Severn Valley Railway, the engine spent many years in steam there until finding a new home at Loughborough in 2001. After another lengthy overhaul No. 46521 re-entered traffic at the end of 2011. (Author)

On 23 April 2015, British Railways Class 9F 2-10-0 No. 92214, masquerading as No. 92220 *Evening Star*, the last steam engine built to work over British Railways lines, in 1960, passes Swithland Sidings Signal box during a special photographic charter event. (Andy Lock)

sections – Loughborough to Quorn; Quorn to Swithland; Swithland to Rothley. It was fitting that the work at Swithland Sidings was awarded a National Railway Heritage Award in December that year.

Understandably, this project dominated media coverage of the Railway's activities, but there were other notable achievements in the second decade of the twenty-first century. In 2011 a 60ft (18.3 metres) locomotive turntable was brought into use at Quorn & Woodhouse Station and in 2013 a major refurbishment of the platform canopies at Loughborough was completed thanks to a very successful £1m public appeal three years earlier.

The latter picked up a National Railway Heritage Award that year in the category 'Station Environment'.

In April 2013 an appeal was successfully launched to fund the building of a four-road carriage shed at Swithland Sidings to house the RVP and the GCR's collections of historic wooden carriages. These plans had superseded those turned down by the local council in the spring of 2007 to build the shed on part of a reinstated Mountsorrel branch running east from Swithland Sidings. Progress on the new shed was rapid, and a completed building was handed over by the erection contractors in July 2014.

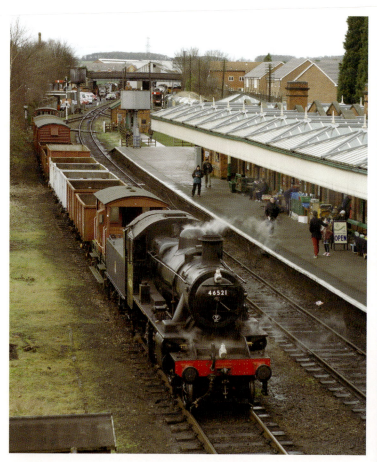

Recreating the feel of a main-line railway of the 1950s took many years of hard and often frustrating work, both physical and mental, from the time enthusiasts first took over a forlorn Loughborough Central Station in 1973 to the scene shown here in 2016. (Author)

A quiet platform two at Loughborough in the year the Station won the 'Station Environment' category of the National Railway Heritage Award. (Author)

Visiting from the preserved Swanage Railway, privately-owned ex-Southern Railway 2-6-0 No. 31806, built in 1928, is pulling away from Loughborough Central Station on the up main line on 31 January 2016. (Author)

The southern approaches to Loughborough Central Station on 8 September 2013. In the middle of the photograph, pulling a diesel multiple unit (DMU) and Class 08 shunter, is preserved Class 47 diesel locomotive D1705, built in 1965, unofficially named *Sparrow Hawk* in 1989, and then again in preservation at Loughborough in June 2004. (Author)

No. 46521 again, this time seen approaching Quorn & Woodhouse Station during the 2016 Spring Gala. (Author)

At the end of January 2016, ex-Southern Railway 2-6-0 No. 31806 from the preserved Swanage Railway worked on the Great Central Railway . It was photographed immediately south of the A6 road bridge outside Loughborough. The original 1890s steel deck of this bridge was replaced in 1994 with the reinforced concrete one seen here. (Author)

Pushing the Boundaries

In that year the Great Central Railway plc achieved a turnover of £2.8m, double what it had been seven years previously when the organisation was struggling financially. Special events, most notably annual galas exploiting the double-track and the loops at Swithland to their maximum were major factors in this improvement. It was a fortunate position to be in, because the railway was about to become involved in three huge expansionist schemes, which would push the boundaries of the organisation to their limits.

The first and, in relation to the other two projects, the most modest, originated with the desire of RVP to build a carriage storage shed on a section of the abandoned Mountsorrel Branch which the organisation owned. Following the failed planning application mentioned above, the reinstatement of the branch took on a life of its own, growing from a purely RVP idea into a wide-ranging community scheme which drew support from the local councils as well as Great Central Railway plc and Lafarge, the owners of the Mountsorrel Works.

After many months of labour by volunteers from all sorts of interested groups, January 2012 witnessed the first steam-hauled mineral train run onto the first section of the restored line, followed on 23 November 2013 by the first passenger-carrying train. The remaining community elements of the project were realised, when in 2014, funds were made available through various initiatives to build the Mountsorrel & Rothley Community Heritage Centre in the former Nunckley Hill Quarry (already designated

Examples of the designs of Sir William Stanier of the London, Midland & Scottish Railway, lined up outside Loughborough Shed at the end of February 2016. On the left is the boiler from No. 48305, an example of his Class 8F 2-8-0 design. In the centre is Black Five 4-6-0 No. 45305, built in 1937. This engine was rescued by A.E. Draper and Sons of Hull, the owners of the yard where it was sent for scrapping, eventually finding its way to Loughborough in 1996. On the right is 8F No. 48624. (Author)

Accelerating past Charnwood Water, south of Loughborough, is visiting locomotive 4-6-2 No. 34053 *Sir Keith Park,* named after the Air Chief Marshal who played such a significant role in Fighter Command and then the defence of Malta during the Second World War. The restoration of this engine after leaving Barry Scrapyard in 1984 proved particularly difficult for a succession of owners. Eventually it was Southern Locomotives Ltd who completed the task in May 2012, sending the locomotive to work on the Severn Valley Railway. (Author)

a Regionally Important Geological Site). Mountsorrel Halt, adjacent to this site, was completed for the official opening of the branch line on 24 October 2015 and the centre itself opened on 25 April 2016.

The other two, much more ambitious, schemes have at the time of writing yet to be delivered. Both involve many different partners and the first to be described is undoubtedly the largest capital project ever attempted on the railway. In October 2004, the National Railway Museum (NRM) opened a new branch museum –'Locomotion' – at Shildon, County Durham, to display some of its collection that could not be seen at its main York site.

Negotiations following this expansion led to the signing in December 2012 of an agreement between the NRM, Leicester City Council and Great Central Railway plc to build a similar branch museum at the railway's southern terminus of Leicester North. For a few people with long memories, the project naturally evoked the ghosts of the stillborn 1988 City Council plans for its own 'Beamish' open-air museum adjacent to the station. The new twenty-first century project was certainly not that. This new museum would require the complete replacement of Leicester North Station. The project was costed at £15m and in order to raise this substantial amount, a submission was made to the Heritage Lottery Fund in November 2013 for £10m against which matching funds could be raised. This initial application to finance preliminary studies, surveys, public and commercial consultations, and numerous other investigations, failed, but a re-submission the following year, for what had by then become 'Main Line Bridging the Nation', was successful. Any project involving HLF money is a lengthy journey and, as this book goes to print, this one still has a long way to go before reaching a conclusion.

The final major scheme involving the railway is in a similar position but with a much lengthier and, problematic, history than either the Mountsorrel Branch or the NRM projects. As mentioned at the beginning of this chapter, the initial aim of the Main Line Preservation Group was to preserve a double-track main line between the outskirts of Nottingham and Leicester. Reality had rapidly reduced this ambition and all efforts were soon concentrated on the line south of Loughborough. However, as long as track remained *in situ* north from

A line-up of locomotives at the northern end of Loughborough Central Station in February 2016. Nearest the camera is Southern Railway 4-6-0 No. 777 *Sir Lamiel*, built in 1925 and a member of the National Collection based at the National Railway Museum, York. The engine arrived at Loughborough in 1995. (Author)

D5401, seen here between Woodthorpe Road Bridge and the A6 bridge at Loughborough, was built in 1962 and put up for sale by British Rail in October 1987. When this photograph was taken in the summer of 2013, the locomotive had been on hire to the Great Central Railway plc since 2009. (Author)

Steaming past Charnwood Water, Loughborough, on a rainy Sunday, 31 January 2016, British Railways Class 9F 2-10-0 No. 92214, dressed up as No. 92220 *Evening Star*, makes an impressive sight with the restored 'Windcutter' train. The 9F moved from the North Yorkshire Moors Railway to Loughborough in January 2014, painted all-over black and bearing the name *Cock o'the North*. It was soon repainted in BR passenger livery and for a short time it was named *Central S*tar. (Author)

Loughborough, and British Rail continued to run trains to and from the MOD depot at Ruddington and British Gypsum at East Leake (Hotchley Hill) via Weekday Cross, Nottingham, hopes lingered that the original vision of the Main Line Steam Trust might be realised some day. That optimism would be severely tested over the next four decades.

Keen to abandon the line into Nottingham because of the many viaducts and bridges that had to be maintained (including the extravagant four-track bridge across the River Trent), at the start of the 1970s British Rail had quickly decided on plans to create a new connection at Loughborough between the former Great Central Railway and the Midland Main Line so that MOD and gypsum trains could reach the national rail network there. It was work on that link undertaken between 1973 and 1975 that materially, and perversely, worsened the preservationists' chances of expanding northwards. To provide material for its new connection, British Rail removed the Great Central Railway embankment between the bridge over the Midland Main Line and that over the Leicester Canal at Loughborough. It was a sensible civil engineering solution, one impossible to have been challenged by a group of railway enthusiasts who in 1973 were busy erecting a locomotive running and maintenance shed over part of the through lines just south of the canal bridge and by 1976 had failed to raise sufficient funds to prevent eight miles of their 'preserved' line being taken up by British Rail.

The canal bridge was allowed to remain, but two others, the most significant being the bridge over the Midland Main Line, were removed, the latter in April 1980. The resultant 'Loughborough gap' became to the Great Central Railway plc what the rubbish-filled cutting at Imberhorne was to the Bluebell Railway in Sussex: an apparently insurmountable barrier to northwards expansion.

The impetus for the first attempt to reconnect the two sections of line came at the end of 1983 when, in October of that year, the MOD Depot at Ruddington closed. The MLST started talks with Rushcliffe Borough Council and BR about a possible purchase of the line from Ruddington to British Gypsum's sidings at Hotchley Hill, near Rushcliffe Halt. The line from there to Loughborough and the junction with the Midland main line was still very occasionally used for gypsum traffic, so there was no immediate threat of the track being lifted on that section. In 1985 a feasibility study was carried out by MLST and Charnwood Borough Council, and talks conducted with other local authorities, with the emphasis on the wider benefits of reuniting the GCR both north and south of Loughborough. The public were made aware of the broad aim of running heritage trains between Ruddington and Leicester North (the Birstall Extension was underway at the time) through exhibitions, leaflets and open days at British Gypsum's sidings, and by the end of 1986, £8,000 had been raised to further the project.

A view looking north from the GCR bridge over the Leicester Canal in 1973 as two JCBs remove the embankment leading to the bridge over the Midland main line at Loughborough. (Author's collection)

At the beginning of 1987, Nottinghamshire County Council announced it would purchase the track between Ruddington and Gotham Moor (a mile north of Hotchley Hill and Rushcliffe Halt) with Rushcliffe Borough Council buying the formation (the trackbed) on that section so that it could be leased back to the MLST. Gotham Moor had been the junction of a branch running west to the gypsum works and it was at that former junction that enthusiasts started to plan for the erection of a shed to house locomotives to work the line to and from Ruddington. But by then their real aspiration was for a railway centre within the grounds of the former MOD depot and the local councils were made aware of this. Consequently, when Nottinghamshire County Council acquired that site in 1989 for reuse as a business and leisure park, it had already taken the enthusiasts' railway-centre plans into consideration.

In October of that year, the Great Central Railway Northern Development Association was created followed shortly afterwards by the incorporation of Great Central Railway (Nottingham) Ltd (GCR(N)). Professional plans of the proposed 'Nottingham Railway Heritage Centre' were presented and accepted by Rushcliffe Borough Council. As work began creating the business and leisure park and the heritage centre, GCR(N), moved some locomotives and rolling stock to British Gypsum's Hotchley Hill sidings in 1990, holding a public open day with one engine in steam there in June that year.

Three years later, the transformed MOD site was transferred to Rushcliffe Borough Council, and the new 'Nottingham Heritage Centre' was officially opened on 10 September 1993. Its original title had been modified to reflect the fact that by then it housed the collections of not only GCR(N) but also Nottingham Area Bus Society and the Nottingham Society of Model & Experimental Engineers Ltd. A few months later, in May the following year, the remainder of the site was opened to the public as Rushcliffe County Park.

In was in this year – 1994 – that the second serious attempt was made to reunite the separated sections of the former GCR either side of Loughborough. In that summer, surveys were carried out around the 'Loughborough Gap' that lead to a number of meetings between Great Central Railway (1976) plc and officers from Nottinghamshire and Leicestershire county councils, Rushcliffe Borough Council and Charnwood Borough Council, to gauge support for reunification. The outcome of the meetings was very positive, and a timetable for 'Bridging the Gap' was drawn up that anticipated that if all the necessary funds were raised, reunification could be achieved to celebrate the 100th anniversary of the opening of the Great Central Railway's main line in March 1899. But this forecast proved too optimistic, as all available resources, financial and physical, were being concentrated on completing the double-track project south of Loughborough, and in Nottinghamshire priorities had already started to change following the privatisation of British Railways in 1994 and British Gypsum's reassessment of the value of its rail connection at Hotchley Hill.

In that year, GCR(N) had started discussions with Railtrack (the rump of British Rail responsible for infrastructure such as track and signalling following privatisation) with the result that in 1997, in a unique arrangement that would never have been possible with the nationalised industry, it took over the maintenance and renewal of the line from Gotham Moor to Loughborough prior to the reintroduction of freight to the East Leake Gypsum Works. This was the first step in GCR(N)'s ultimate aim of an outright purchase of the line from Railtrack.

Major track upgrading was undertaken and, on 1 December 1998, the first freight arrived at British Gypsum's Hotchley Hill sidings from off the national rail network at Loughborough. That soon led to an intensive, regular service that was not merely a reintroduction of what British Gypsum had abandoned in the 1980s. To feed an enlarged and modernised manufacturing facility at East Leake, an almost daily flow of gypsum was about to start running, brought in by rail from the coal-fired power stations at West Burton, Cottam and Drax, where it had been created as a waste product.

The reintroduction of freight services obviously complicated plans to run heritage trains from the Heritage Centre into Rushcliffe Halt. It was also a considerable hindrance to the aim of running all the way to the outskirts of Loughborough and, ultimately, to the aspirations of through running between Ruddington and Leicester North. In 1995 GCR(N) purchased Nottinghamshire County Council's section of line southwards from Ruddington to Gotham Moor and from 17 October 1999, it was able to start a regular public service between the Heritage Centre and Gotham Moor. However, more negotiations were needed with Railtrack before any trains could reach Rushcliffe Halt. This was eventually achieved in June 2000 and although GCR(N) finally completed the purchase of all the remaining track southwards to Loughborough the following year, it was not until 2003 that regular passenger-carrying trains were able to use the whole length of the line between the Heritage Centre and Loughborough. Passengers could neither alight nor join trains at the latter place, and those trains were only able to run at weekends, leaving the route clear for freight during the week, but nevertheless it was a huge achievement.

The preserved prototype High Speed Train (HST) driving unit along with three appropriate Mark III carriages enter Rushcliffe Halt on a bitterly cold St Valentine Day Sunday, 2016. The Station opened on 5 June 1911 as Rushcliffe Platform and remained open until the beginning of March 1963. The platform shelters seen in this photograph were erected during 2012. British Gypsum's East Leake Works and headquarters are in the background. (Author)

The Elizabethan
Sunday Luncheon Dining Train carefully pulling into Rothley Station on 13 March 2016. From the earliest days of preservation, special dining trains were seen by many heritage lines as a way of generating both extra income and interest from those who were not necessarily 'railway enthusiasts'. This particular service was introduced in 2003. The impressive lattice post signal behind the train came from Uttoxeter and was re-erected as Rothley's up home signal in May 2008. (Author)

A view from Beeches Road Bridge looking towards Loughborough Central Station, as London, Midland & Scottish Railway Class 8F 2-8-0 No. 48624 accelerates away with a 'Windcutter' on 31 January 2016. This locomotive was restored over a twenty-eight-year period by tenacious enthusiasts, steaming first at the preserved Peak Rail line in Derbyshire in 2009 before working over the Great Central Railway plc route in 2011. (Author)

The view looking north from Quorn & Woodhouse Station on 31 January 2016, with *Sir Keith Park* and No. 31806 double-heading an afternoon train. It is a testament to the hard work over many years by so many people that compelling scenes like this have been made possible.(Author)

Another shot in January 2016 rain with *Witherslack Hall* hauling mixed freight out of Loughborough and passing *Sir Lamiel* in the up siding waiting its next turn. (Author)

Bridge to the Future

With trains finally arriving from the north within whistling distance of Loughborough Central Station, it was time once again to pursue that seemingly impossible, and certainly elusive, goal of reunification. Extra impetus also came because an announcement was imminent about the electrification of the Midland Main Line that would have a crucial impact on whether or not a replacement bridge could be erected over that line at Loughborough.

At the end of 2007, estimates of £6m to achieve reunification were made public, and in 2010 Great Central Railway Development Ltd (GCRD) was formed to drive forward a new scheme, which, interestingly, listed the reinstatement of the Mountsorrel Branch and the creation of an out-station of the NRM at Leicester North as key components. The goals of reunification were stated as the creation of the long hoped for 'inter-city' heritage railway link between Nottingham and Leicester, access from the national rail network at Loughborough to the planned NRM out-station at Leicester North, and a new route for stone quarried by Lafarge at Mountsorrel to the national rail network. This latter proposal, controversial, but with the prospect of bringing extra funding to the whole project, called for the reinstatement of the Mountsorrel Branch to a standard capable of taking heavy mineral trains, a new east to north link at Swithland Sidings and the upgrading of the existing preserved line from there to Loughborough where the stone trains would cross the Midland Main Line before reversing to join it using the 1975 link.

Another crucial consideration in any reunification plan was what track layout should be laid between Empress Road Bridge, just north of Loughborough Central Station, and the canal bridge. As mentioned elsewhere, in 1973 the preservationists had erected their locomotive shed across the former running lines in this section. Although there was space on the western side of the shed to lay a single track, the preferred option was to reinstate the running lines on their original alignment and either move the existing shed or build a new one elsewhere. Just before GCRD was created, a proper motive power depot (MPD) had been planned on land north-east of where the former GCR embankment had been removed in 1973/4, but, unfortunately, the initiative had foundered.

By the start of 2013, reinstatement of the Mountsorrel Branch for stone traffic was no longer part of the GCRD's plans and in May that year Network Rail (formed in 2002 as the successor to Railtrack) announced it would erect the new Loughborough Bridge as part of its electrification project, using two concrete and steel spans recovered from work at Reading, and already donated to the preservationists. The bridge work was costed at £1m, a fraction of what some had estimated, so GCRD immediately launched its 'Bridge to the Future' appeal to raise that amount. If it could be raised, then completion was scheduled for the following year.

Inevitably there was slippage. Planning permission was granted in June 2014 by which time half a million pounds had been donated from enthusiasts all over the country. Taking advantage of a new deadline – the summer of 2015 – the scheme was 'refined', and by the end of the year the plan was to fabricate a completely new, single-span structure to cross the Midland Main Line and use the Reading bridges as part of a new viaduct instead of an earth embankment immediately south of the new main-line bridge.

All the necessary studies and permissions were in place, and, with funds still pouring in, everyone was more optimistic than before that this particular scheme would be successful in reunifying

The first phase of the Loughborough 'Bridging the Gap' project starts immediately to the east of the Midland Main Line in February 2016. (Author)

the two sections of former GCR main line. But it was not to be, because of an unexpected Government decision. In June 2015, the Government announced it was 'pausing' the Midland Main Line electrification. Network Rail no longer had a scheme into which it could dovetail the Loughborough bridge work. It was a bitter moment, especially as there was by then £950,000 already in the bank.

After a period of heart-searching, the GCDR and all those involved in the project agreed to soldier on. No longer the main contractor, Network Rail remained supportive and when electrification was 'un-paused' in September, everyone was ready to embrace another set of deadlines: electric trains between Bedford and Kettering (and Corby) by 2019, and then onwards to Leicester, Nottingham and Sheffield by 2023. At the end of 2015 the by-then merely symbolic £1m target was reached, and on 12 February the following year, the official 'first sod' of the 'Bridge to the Future' was cut by Loughborough's MP, Nicky Morgan. This was the beginning of yet another saga in the history of the Great Central Railway that, at the time of writing, has still to reach its conclusion.

Photographed shortly after entering traffic at the end of 1947, LNER Class B1 No. 1248 *Geoffrey Gibbs* crosses the former Midland Railway main line at Loughborough with a northbound freight. (Neville Stead)

Index

(photograph page numbers in **bold**)

Bibliography

The following is not a definitive list of all the books that have been written about the Great Central Railway, but a list of those used as references in the compilation of this book:

'Trains Illustrated, British Railways Then & Now: no.11 The Great Central', Basil Cooper, Ian Allan Publishing, nd

'Great Central Vol.1', George Dow, Locomotive Publishing Co., 1959

'Great Central Vol.2', George Dow, Locomotive Publishing Co., 1962

'Great Central Vol.3', George Dow, Ian Allan Publishing, 1965

'Great Central Album', George Dow, Ian Allan Publishing, 1969

'Great Central Recalled', George Dow, Bradford Barton Ltd, 1978

'The Cheshire Lines Committee', Nigel Dyckhoff, Ian Allan Publishing, 1984

'Portrait of the Cheshire Lines Committee', Nigel Dyckhoff, Ian Allan Publishing, 1999

'The Final Link', D. Edwards & Ron Pigram, Midas Books, 1982

'The Great Central Then & Now', Mac Hawkins, David & Charles, 1991

'Great Central Memories', J.M.C. Healy, Barton Transport, 1987

'Echoes of the Great Central', J.M.C. Healy, Oxford Publishing Company, 1987

'William Bradshaw Leicester Railway Cameraman 1909–1923', J. Hurst & M. Kinder, The Historical Model Railway Society, 2002

'Scenes from the Past No.29: Woodhead (Part One)', E.M. Johnson, Foxline Publishing, 1996

'Scenes from the Past No.29: Woodhead (Part Two)', E.M. Johnson, Foxline Publishing, nd

'The Last Main Line', Leicester Museums, 1968

'Great Central Railway's London Extension', Robert Robotham, Ian Allan Publishing, 1999

'The Making of a Railway', L.T.C. Rolt, H. Evelyn, 1971

'Main Line Lament: The Final Years of the Great Central route to London', Colin Walker, Oxford Publishing Co., 1973

'Great Central Twilight: Memories of a lost main line to London', Colin Walker, Pendyke Publications, 1986